Family Planning

Establishing Goals and Fostering Family Success

(An in-depth Guide Book on the Fertility Awareness Method on How to Expect the Unexpected)

James Cabezas

Published By **Oliver Leish**

James Cabezas

All Rights Reserved

Family Planning: Establishing Goals and Fostering Family Success (An in-depth Guide Book on the Fertility Awareness Method on How to Expect the Unexpected)

ISBN 978-0-9867663-0-5

No part of this guidebook shall be reproduced in any form without permission in writing from the publisher except in the case of brief quotations embodied in critical articles or reviews.

Legal & Disclaimer

The information contained in this book is not designed to replace or take the place of any form of medicine or professional medical advice. The information in this book has been provided for educational & entertainment purposes only.

The information contained in this book has been compiled from sources deemed reliable, and it is accurate to the best of the Author's knowledge; however, the Author cannot guarantee its accuracy and validity and cannot be held liable for any errors or omissions. Changes are periodically made to this book. You must consult your doctor or get professional medical advice before using any of the suggested remedies, techniques, or information in this book.

Upon using the information contained in this book, you agree to hold harmless the Author from and against any damages, costs, and expenses, including any legal fees potentially resulting from the application of any of the information provided by this guide. This disclaimer applies to any damages or injury caused by the use and application, whether directly or indirectly, of any advice or information presented, whether for breach of contract, tort, negligence, personal injury, criminal intent, or under any other cause of action.

You agree to accept all risks of using the information presented inside this book. You need to consult a professional medical practitioner in order to ensure you are both able and healthy enough to participate in this program.

Table Of Contents

Chapter 1: The Power Of The Family Plan 1

Chapter 2: The Importance Of Goals 15

Chapter 3: Introducing Family Meetings 29

Chapter 4: The Importance Of Communication 57

Chapter 5: Creating The Family Vision ... 74

Chapter 6: Setting Individual Goals 82

Chapter 7: From Goals To Plans- Creating A Personal Blueprint 90

Chapter 8: Building The Family Plan Blueprint 104

Chapter 9: Turning Goals Into Action ... 116

Chapter 10: Nurturing Persistence And Resilience 127

Chapter 11: The Ongoing Process 141

Chapter 12: What Are Family Planning Methods? 149

Chapter 13: Permanent Family Planning Methods 175

Chapter 1: The Power Of The Family Plan

Imagine being on a battlefield, a big, chaotic landscape full of uncertainty and danger. Survival is the remaining motive, but how does one continue to exist without a plan, without any easy commands or hints?

Imagine each soldier wandering spherical aimlessly, without a map, compass, or radio conversation. No knowledge of the task or the enemy, and no coordination with their fellow squaddies. They are in essence, lone wolves, every searching out to stay on, but extra often than now not, strolling headfirst into threat without even facts it.

That's a catastrophe equipped to show up, isn't it? This is exactly what takes vicinity whilst a own family attempts to navigate lifestyles's annoying conditions with out a stable plan - a 'Family Plan'. Without smooth desires, effective communique, and a shared vision, family participants can also moreover locate themselves metaphorically wandering aimlessly on their personal non-public battlefields, each seeking to live on, however without any feel of direction or coordinated help from the team, the family.

This is why we need a Family Plan, a technique to manual each member and the own family as a whole towards collective achievement. In this ebook, we're going to learn how to draw up this crucial plan, leveraging my decade-prolonged experience as a bomb technician in the US Army, and my years counseling and guiding infantrymen and their families to create a fixed up, smooth, and effective blueprint for family success.

The Family Plan is a powerful, three-element approach designed to manual every family member and the family unit as a whole, in the direction of success. The 3 crucial factors of the Family Plan are Mindset, Behavior/Habits, and the Written Plan.

Mindset is the the use of stress, the strength of mind that galvanizes the family to return lower returned together, determine to a weekly meeting, and foster a shared desire to develop and be successful collectively. It's the mental gasoline propelling us to step out of our consolation zones and embody alternate for the higher.

Behavior/Habits function the tangible expressions of our thoughts-set, becoming visible through our repeated actions. These behaviors steadily form us and our relationships. Throughout this ebook, I purposefully emphasize certain regular requirements and ideas. You'll be aware this as we revisit the importance of cultivating optimistic habits, which incorporates preserving regular circle of relatives meetings and running closer to powerful self-conversation.

This repetition is intentional, because it takes a normal reminder of these middle ideas to embed them into each your aware and subconscious mind. Just as our conduct are customary and bolstered through repeated movements, those vital mind want not unusual revisiting to come to be a herbal part of our circle of relatives thoughts-set and behaviors. Through this plan, our intention is that will help you set up and nurture the ones essential behavior, thereby fostering a stronger, greater harmonious circle of relatives unit.

Finally, we've got were given the Written Plan. This is a important element, and you may soon see why it's far vital that it's far physical written and not digital. Many research and real-life testimonies display the remarkable strength of writing down desires. The easy act of writing your dreams makes you forty seven% much more likely to be successful. But we're aiming for more than that. We're aiming for an entire, nicely-articulated roadmap to carrying out your desires.

Why is writing so effective? It leverages the may additionally additionally of visualization. Your mind is an exquisite powerhouse, and hundreds of its hobby takes location subconsciously, past your immediately manipulate. In essence, your aware mind sets the diploma for what your subconscious mind prioritizes, second excellent to your vital survival wishes.

In our every day life, our minds are bombarded with infinite subjects to attention on, taking in thousands and heaps of character information factors. It's our subconscious that kinds via this information, on the same time as we pass approximately our routine sports. This is why proper intentions, like New Year's resolutions or fitness center memberships, often get sidetracked. It's smooth to be derailed by means of way of different unconscious priorities until our desires are embedded in our conscious popularity. That's in which the Written Plan, or the Blueprint to Success, is available in.

When we physical write down our goals and map out the stairs to gain them, we create a effective device for harnessing our subconscious mind. By posting this seen reminder at the wall, we are signaling to our unconscious mind what our priorities are. We are maintaining our dedication to the ones desires, preserving them sparkling in our minds, and continuously nudging our unconscious to keep them at the forefront of our priorities.

Why does this consider? Why can we want a Family Plan? You might be asking your self these questions as you dive into this e-book. To solution, allow's take a second and go searching. Many households, likely which include yours, may additionally have a indistinct concept in their dreams, but now not a definitive, actionable plan.

Reflect for a second. When have become the remaining time you had a circle of relatives assembly? When did you final sit down down alongside facet your companion and ask about their dreams? Or even make an effort to ask your self approximately your non-public goals? Did you jot down a few issue? If you probable did, was it only a smooth 'to-do' listing?

While 'to-do' lists are higher than not having any route in any respect, they regularly fall brief as an powerful motion plan. What's more, they're able to grow to be a supply of pressure, particularly at the same time as devices continue to be unchecked for lengthy durations. It feels actual to acquire a list, however the pleasure fades when you cannot complete the obligations, growing a awful feedback loop. Your unconscious mind, ever keen to avoid ache, can also moreover additionally start to influence you some distance from the list, and the related horrible feelings it induces.

We understand that families in recent times are extra occupied than ever. Juggling artwork, circle of relatives chores, college, extracurricular sports activities activities, and social commitments can depart little time for collective making plans. The regular hustle of cutting-edge existence, intensified by means of using economic pressures, makes it difficult to synchronize everybody's efforts. But the adventure to achievement starts offevolved offevolved with a unmarried step, and it does not should be a big soar. Remember, small, constant steps can result in huge exchange.

So, how will the Written Family Plan benefit you and your family? Let's delve deeper into that in the next segment.

The Family Plan is greater than simplest a structural detail on your circle of relatives; it is a tool with numerous benefits which could beautify your circle of relatives lifestyles in hundreds of strategies. Let's test a number of the vital factor benefits that enforcing the Family Plan can keep on your family.

1. Enhanced Communication: One of the most obvious advantages of the Family Plan is the improvement in verbal exchange amongst family individuals. Regular circle of relatives conferences, scheduled as quickly as every week to begin with, provide a platform for anybody to explicit their mind, mind, and

concerns overtly. Over time, the ones conferences becomes a loved lifestyle, fostering consider, know-how, and a shared experience of motive inside the circle of relatives.

2. Effective Goal-Setting and Tracking: With the Family Plan, aim-setting becomes a extra established and precise method. By contrary-engineering goals into actionable steps, every family member might also have a smooth course to examine, removing ambiguity and boosting motivation. Additionally, tracking those desires becomes extra attainable even as they may be damaged down into smaller, manageable steps, thereby building a enjoy of feat and improvement.

3. Tangible Written Plan: The act of physical writing desires triggers a unique cognitive effect. Your mind interprets those written goals in a wonderful way than fleeting thoughts or spoken terms. It perceives the written desires as a willpower and focuses its

electricity on devising strategies to benefit them, rather than sincerely retaining song of them.

four. Develops Critical Thinking and Problem-Solving Skills: Engaging in the Family Plan machine is not clearly about setting and attractive in desires; it is also an exercising in growing essential thinking and problem-solving skills. As the circle of relatives collaborates to acquire their plan, each member, irrespective of age, can make contributions their particular mind-set to conquer traumatic conditions and devise solutions. These capabilities, honed in the protection of the own family, may be applied to all components of existence, equipping own family members with the resilience and flexibility needed in an ever-changing worldwide.

These are only a few of the benefits your family can achieve from imposing the Family Plan. As we delve deeper into the ebook, we're going to discover the ones advantages in greater detail and provide you with actionable strategies to apprehend them in your family.

This ebook serves as a complete manual, providing you the gadget, strategies, and insights vital to create and put into effect your personal Family Plan. It's designed to make the procedure now not simplest possible however furthermore exciting and fun for all circle of relatives humans.

Each financial disaster is dedicated to a selected component of the Family Plan, unfolding the manner in a step-thru-step manner, ensuring that no stone is left unturned. As we journey collectively thru this ebook, you may learn how to installation easy, feasible goals for both individuals and the family as an entire. We will dive deep into the artwork of effective conversation and its critical function in fortifying familial relationships and making your Family Plan a success.

In this ebook, we're going to guide you via numerous key steps. First, we will help you create a shared vision that your entire circle of relatives can get inside the again of. Then, every member of the family will make their personal private plan and set character dreams. Together, you may integrate these into a unmarried Family Plan.

Next, we are going to show you ways to reveal the ones plans and dreams into real movements that you may begin proper away. We'll also teach you the manner to run circle of relatives meetings that assist anyone live heading within the proper direction and guide every other.

Finally, we're going to discover strategies to preserve going on the same time as matters get difficult. You'll discover ways to bring together staying electricity and resilience in your circle of relatives so you can keep making development, no matter what demanding situations get up.

This e-book isn't always absolutely a theoretical exploration of these topics, but it gives practical, actionable steps that you may start imposing right now. These techniques are complemented via actual-life examples and practical physical sports activities that will help you recognize and practice the necessities effectively.

By the time you end studying, you may no longer first-class have an in depth facts of the Family Plan but in reality have a smooth route to enforce it in your own family. You'll be equipped with the facts and strategies to show your own family proper right into a goal-orientated, communique-green, and harmonious unit this is ready to take on the annoying conditions and joys of life collectively.

So, allow's embark on this exciting journey to create your Family Plan, reworking the dynamics of your circle of relatives, one cause at a time. Stay with us; you're approximately to investigate, grow, and be successful collectively as a own family.

As you delve into the imminent chapters, you may advantage the know-how, equipment, and techniques you want to make your Family Plan a fact. Each bankruptcy is a leap ahead, guiding you in growing and carrying out your awesome blueprint. This consists of personal blueprints for each family member, vision forums, and in the long run, your blended own family plan.

But remember, records with out software program is simply facts. It's the movement you take, the adjustments you positioned into effect, and the persistence you display that lets in you to without a doubt bring about transformation.

Chapter 2: The Importance Of Goals

When it includes attaining any huge transformation, success in any undertaking, or riding great exchange in a family setting, the magic all boils proper right down to setting the proper desires. Goals shape the compass that gives your own family with a revel in of course and motive. They aren't first-rate a forestall line but moreover the roadmap that plots out the adventure within the direction of that line. However, the software of goals extends beyond being mere navigation gear. They act as yardsticks that assist you to song your development, degree your strides, and make crucial adjustments alongside the manner.

But placing goals is handiest the start of the journey. Realization of these goals isn't a rely of wishful thinking or easy assertion. Goals, in particular massive ones, are rarely accomplished in one fell swoop. They require committed strive, systematic making plans, and a divide-and-triumph over technique.

Hence, the essence of breaking them down into potential, actionable steps.

Consider this analogy: If you have been to construct a residence, you will not in truth turn up at an empty lot in the destiny, armed with a pile of wooden and a toolbox, and expect everything to fall into area. Instead, you can depend on a blueprint—an in depth plan that publications each hammer swing, every noticed lessen, and every nail pushed, subsequently turning the pile of wood proper proper into a beautiful, livable domestic.

Your own family's desires require a similar technique. To flip your desires into realities, you need a whole plan—a blueprint that no longer most effective outlines the very last intention however moreover charts the route to wearing out it, little by little. This blueprint starts offevolved offevolved with expertise a way to deconstruct your dreams into practicable steps, and this is what we can discover in this economic ruin. By the give up of this journey, you will have a smooth course, a systematic technique, and an actionable plan to manual your circle of relatives closer to your collective dreams.

Our verbal exchange approximately desires and the way of breaking them down into smaller, actionable steps may additionally moreover have left you thinking, "What does that genuinely seem like—and the way do I do it?" To assist you visualize and plan out your family's journey, permit's stroll via a simple workout. We'll use "being profitable as a Real Estate agent" as an instance to demonstrate the gadget, but the steps can be tailor-made to any motive your family has. Remember, this exercising serves as just a model. Your Blueprint may be honestly unique on your family, and you can format it in any manner you see healthy. The essential thing is that you make investments time to physical write out your goals, breaking them down into possible steps. This is the essence of creating your aspirations tangible and putting your family at the route to shared success.

Let's begin.

Step 1: Grab a easy piece of paper/poster board and a few issue to put in writing with.

Step 2: Position the paper horizontally.

Step 3: In the top right corner of the paper, write down your closing purpose. For many, this might be some problem like "Financial Freedom," because it shows safety on your family and the liberty to pursue different passions and duties. However, this may be some aspect which you and your circle of relatives aspire to benefit. Be tremendous to function your call within the pinnacle left and you can use the higher middle vicinity for notes or motivational expenses and so forth...

Step 4: On the a protracted way right facet of the paper, right away below your final cause, listing a few sub-desires that contribute on your primary intention. In our example, we might write "Become a Successful Real Estate Agent" thinking about that that could be a method to gain our very last intention of economic freedom. Underneath this sub-purpose, jot down some bullet factors describing what you envision to be right about this goal within the destiny. At this point, you can additionally draw packing containers spherical your dreams to effortlessly distinguish them.

Step five: Now, on foot from right to left, next to the Real Estate sub-purpose, write what desires to be actual just in advance than this sub-purpose can arise. For example, "Sell 10 Homes in line with Month." Underneath this, listing bullet elements of ideas or what wishes to be real to acquire this step. If you're uncertain, mark a massive query mark ("?") indicating that you want to research similarly. In our instance, we would write, "Generate 3 hundred Leads in step with Month."

Step 6: Keep walking left to right, breaking down your sub-desires into smaller segments, until you can't think about some aspect else.

Step 8: Review your contrary-engineered Sub-Goals and choose out each day and weekly duties which will assist obtain those mini-segments. Write the ones obligations down on the an extended manner left detail or your Blueprint. For example, "create 3 social media posts in keeping with day," "observe up with 20 leads in step with day," and so forth. These responsibilities ought to additionally be transferred to a every day planner and reviewed/updated frequently as your plan adapts and responsibilities are finished.

As you whole this workout, you could start to see why a plan, or a "Blueprint"/"Family Plan," is so important. It takes your overarching aim and breaks it down into steps, transforming an summary aim proper proper right into a concrete movement plan. Instead of a indistinct to-do listing access like "Make coins with Real Estate," you presently have a comprehensive manner that shows you the right steps you need to take to understand your dreams. This underlines the profound significance and power of crafting a Blueprint, which in the long run bureaucracy the spine of your Family Plan.

If you mirror at the exercising we simply completed, you may understand that our closing purpose—financial freedom— felt significantly greater ability as quickly as we broke it down into feasible steps. But why is this way so powerful?

The solution lies within the intersection of cognitive psychology and motivation precept. When you truly preserve your purpose as a highbrow idea or depend on a easy to-do list, it could experience daunting and nebulous. The end goal may additionally additionally appear some distance away or maybe no longer viable, and it could be tough to appearance a smooth direction to venture it. This perceived lack of development can be demotivating, leading to procrastination or leaving inside the back of the motive surely.

On the alternative, breaking down your aim into smaller, feasible steps makes the quit objective enjoy greater conceivable. This is a highbrow precept referred to as 'chunking,' which suggests that our brains can extra with out problems device and reap duties while they may be divided into smaller, possible chunks.

In the context of our goals, breaking them down into smaller steps makes the obligations seem much less intimidating. As you start to check off those smaller steps, you'll enjoy a experience of development and fulfillment, imparting a motivational decorate that propels you in addition towards your final intention.

Moreover, writing down your dreams and the steps you need to take to accumulate them reinforces their importance in your mind. According to Dr. Gail Matthews, a psychology professor at the Dominican University in California, you are forty two% much more likely to acquire your goals if you write them down. Writing them down creates a physical report of your purpose and keeps you accountable.

In essence, breaking down goals into viable steps leverages our cognitive dispositions to help us live inspired, make progress, and in the long run benefit our desires. It is an essential part of the motive-putting and fulfillment approach, and some component we need to all encompass into our Family Plans.

Daily and Weekly Tasks

Having laid out the advantages and significance of breaking down dreams, allow's now delve deeper into the identification and incorporation of each day and weekly obligations into your habitual. These obligations are the constructing blocks of your closing purpose, and setting them into practice is the actual recreation-changer.

The functionality to apprehend these obligations comes from the meticulous contrary engineering of our most essential intention into sub-goals, after which in addition into character segments. This technique essentially offers us a clean roadmap towards our final motive, making the adventure heaps a great deal less daunting and more conceivable. In reality, without the Blueprint and the opposite engineering approach, identifying daily or weekly obligations is probably an extremely good, if no longer now not feasible, project.

Once you have got diagnosed the ones obligations, it's miles critical to comprise them into your each day existence. It's no longer enough to simply comprehend what those duties are—you need to take energetic steps to execute them. This is wherein making plans comes into play. By consciously dedicating time to those obligations for your agenda, you take control of your aim success technique. If you are now not already doing this, now could be the time to begin cultivating this dependancy.

A planner may be a precious device for this motive. We recommend that every member of the family ought to have their private planner. It's not pretty a incredible deal having a place to put in writing down your responsibilities—it's miles approximately having a personal, tangible reminder of your desires which you bring with you each day. This can be surprisingly motivating, and it can hold you at the proper track and shifting in advance.

However, it is important to consider that your planner is a manual, not a supply of stress. Don't get discouraged if you're not succesful to complete all of the obligations you have got indexed for a given day. Instead, treat this as an opportunity to check and alter. Maybe you are giving your self too many duties consistent with day? Start small, frequently increase your load, and hold in thoughts that this device is as masses approximately constructing behavior of success as it is approximately sporting out your precise desires.

In essence, identifying and incorporating day by day and weekly duties into your normal transforms your final reason from an summary concept into a sensible, conceivable objective. It's about taking action, staying prompted, and most significantly, making regular development closer to your circle of relatives's collective achievement.

We've included loads in this bankruptcy, delving deep into the concept of the Blueprint and the method of breaking down a Main Goal into Sub-Goals, and further down into Daily and Weekly obligations. Each step of the manner, we've emphasized the want to make our hobbies tangible, possible, and embedded in our each day workout routines.

The Blueprint isn't always only a concept or a metaphor; it is a practical device to guide your adventure inside the route of your circle of relatives's collective success. It takes your Ultimate Goal, a massive aspiration, and breaks it down into smaller, concrete steps. This technique enables to take away the overwhelming feeling regularly related to pursuing a large aim, making it extra approachable and doable.

Incorporating a every day planner into this machine serves to hold you on route, embedding your cause-related duties into your day by day lifestyles. It enables assemble the addiction of useful movement, grade by grade shaping your regular ordinary within the direction of engaging in your Ultimate Goal. But remember, statistics without motion is without a doubt information. It's vital which you exercise developing your personal Blueprint, from the Main Goal via the Sub-Goals and all the way down to the Daily and Weekly responsibilities, using a planner to keep you responsible and on the proper song.

Having your very personal Blueprint previous to moving on to the following monetary smash is important as you will be main the fee in bringing the family together to create a collective Family Plan. It's a good deal lots much less complicated to manual others thru a gadget that you've professional and understood your self.

Here's a in addition illustration of the manner a "Blueprint" might be dependent, you can upload as plenty or as little element as you need.

As we transition into the following financial disaster, we're capable of start to find out the significance of 'Family Meetings', a platform in which each family member may be encouraged to create their very personal individual Blueprint. These meetings can even function a area for collective talk and coordination, evolving the man or woman plans right right into a cohesive Family Plan.

In the subsequent chapters, the private revel in of making your personal Blueprint can be beneficial. It will not most effective assist you to be a higher manual on your family individuals but moreover will let you deliver an motive of the reasoning and blessings inside the lower back of each step. So permit's skip earlier, geared up with our Blueprints, equipped to convey the own family together in pursuit of our collective success.

Chapter 3: Introducing Family Meetings

In this chapter, we can introduce the idea of circle of relatives conferences, a critical element within the development and maintenance of your circle of relatives plan. The concept of a circle of relatives meeting may also sound overly formal or maybe useless, but even as you begin to recognize their rate, they come to be an vital device for the cohesive functioning of a family.

Family conferences, at their center, are scheduled times in which absolutely everyone come collectively to talk approximately, plan, and put together around their collective and character goals. Much like a commercial employer meeting, a own family assembly offers a based time and area for open speak, targeted discussion, and energetic making plans. However, the ones aren't as rigid as business organisation conferences and go away masses of room for warmth, records, and empathy, reflecting the essence of a circle of relatives.

Having normal own family conferences has multiple advantages. Firstly, they offer all people with an facts of what is taking region at a broader own family stage. It is probably plans for a vacation, budgeting selections, or development within the path of the general own family goals. With every person on the same web web page, you're more likely to characteristic cohesively and make alternatives that replicate the remarkable pastimes of all individuals.

Secondly, those meetings make certain that everyone is aligned with the family's desires. It gives a platform for each member of the family to proportion their mind, ideas, and worries. This way, all voices are heard, and all of us feels worried in shaping the family's future.

Lastly, circle of relatives meetings become a manner of obligation. If a family member commits to a challenge or intention at some point of the assembly, they will be much more likely to have a have a look at via statistics that progress might be reviewed within the next meeting. It creates a revel in of obligation and may be a sturdy motivator towards conducting duties and task goals.

In the following sections, we are going to delve deeper into the realistic factors of organizing those conferences, coping with ability resistance, and making them a great and effective experience for all people worried. But for now, it is critical to apprehend and recognize the fee of circle of relatives meetings and their primary characteristic in the a success implementation of your own family plan.

Overcoming Resistance

Despite the numerous benefits of circle of relatives meetings, it is natural to stumble upon some preliminary resistance to this new habitual. People may be hesitant about alternate, particularly on the same time as it comes with a degree of willpower and calls for day trip of their already busy schedules. Moreover, for some, the concept of based totally totally circle of relatives meetings may also appear overly formal or restrictive.

That stated, resistance want to now not discourage you from installing this vital habitual for the betterment of your circle of relatives. Instead, view this as an possibility to engage in substantial conversations, easy misunderstandings, and discover a common floor that everyone can agree upon.

The first step in overcoming resistance is making sure anyone is aware the motive and benefits of these meetings. Explain that the ones are not alleged to be stiff boardroom-style gatherings but instead an possibility for the own family to bond, percentage their thoughts, and artwork collaboratively inside the direction in their desires. These meetings are intended to improve communique, offer assist, and beautify the overall own family dynamic.

Another powerful method is to start slow. Instead of insisting on extended, formal conferences from the get-bypass, begin with short, casual conferences which might be extra dialogue-orientated as opposed to mission-orientated. As your circle of relatives turns into extra cushty with the machine, you could step by step introduce greater form and aim-oriented discussions. Starting slow lets in all people to regulate to the idea and spot the blessings firsthand, with out feeling overwhelmed.

Finally, take some time to deal with character issues. If a family member is resistant, engage them in a one-on-one speak to apprehend their hesitation. It is probably that they feel too forced, or they may be involved about the time self-control, or they could genuinely feel uncomfortable discussing their dreams with the family. Once you apprehend their troubles, you may modify the technique to reason them to revel in greater cushty. Remember, the purpose of these conferences is to sell brotherly love and collaboration, not to create anxiety.

In the subsequent sections, we are going to discover the unique additives of a a hit family assembly, from setting an time table to celebrating successes. For now, recall that the purpose is to get anybody on board with an open mind and a inclined spirit. Patience, facts, and versatility are key on this preliminary segment.

Structuring Family Meetings

Once everybody within the own family is on board with the idea of everyday conferences, the following step is to set up a shape for those gatherings. Having a installed meeting no longer simplest continues the verbal exchange centered and efficient but moreover guarantees that everyone's time is legitimate. Here are some key elements to don't forget whilst structuring your family conferences:

Frequency: Depending on your own family's wishes and schedules, you could decide to maintain the ones meetings weekly or month-to-month. Weekly conferences allow for more immediately comments and faster direction correction if wanted. Monthly meetings is probably greater appropriate if your desires are longer-time period and do now not require weekly adjustments. The vital aspect is to set up a ordinary cadence that everyone can decide to.

Duration: Respect anyone's time through way of putting and sticking to a selected duration. Meetings which might be too lengthy can end up tiring and lose their effectiveness. Aim for 30 to 60 mins, relying on the complexity of the issues being mentioned.

Progress Updates: Each assembly should encompass a section for improvement updates. This is while each member of the family shares their development toward their man or woman desires and the own family purpose. It's an possibility to talk approximately what's operating, what's no longer, and what modifications need to be made.

Problem-Solving: If a member of the family is encountering demanding situations in reaching their goals, the own family assembly is a really perfect time to speak about those boundaries and brainstorm solutions. Remember, the motive of those meetings isn't always responsible or criticize however to help each distinctive in achieving their desires.

Celebrating Successes: Celebrate each big and small victories. Recognizing successes, regardless of how small, boosts morale and keeps all people recommended. So, ensure to consist of a phase in your assembly to famend and have fun the improvement made.

Planning for the Future: Finally, commit a part of the assembly to talk approximately destiny plans. This can include placing new goals, discussing upcoming demanding situations, or making plans for precise activities.

Remember, the purpose of the family assembly isn't to characteristic every other chore in your time desk. Instead, it have to be a time of bonding, mutual useful resource, and improvement inside the course of shared and character goals. In the following sections, we are able to speak more about trouble-solving sooner or later of circle of relatives conferences and the significance of celebrating successes. But for now, use the ones hints to start structuring your family conferences in a way that works notable on your family.

Establishing Ground Rules

Just because it's critical to have a form in your family meetings, it's similarly essential to installation some ground regulations. These guidelines set the tone for the way the assembly will proceed and help create a secure and respectful region for anybody. Let's talk a few crucial floor guidelines you can want to remember:

Active Listening: The first rule to put in force is energetic listening. This technique that once someone is speaking, anybody else have to be definitely present and focused on what's being stated, with out interruption. Active listening additionally includes responding to the speaker in a manner that indicates you apprehend their attitude, which may be accomplished with the aid of summarizing or paraphrasing what they've said or asking clarifying questions. This demonstrates admire for the speaker's perspectives and lets in make certain that everybody feels heard and understood.

Example: If your teenage daughter is expressing her worrying situations with managing time for studies and chores, you could reply with some thing like, "So, what I'm hearing is that you're finding it difficult to stability your schoolwork and your responsibilities at domestic. Is that proper?"

Respectful Communication: The 2d rule is to ensure all communication is respectful. This consists of retaining off awful language, criticism, or blame. Instead, use first-rate, optimistic language and cognizance on answers in vicinity of troubles.

Example: Instead of saying, "You in no manner assist with the dishes," say, "It is probably in fact beneficial if you could help with the dishes after dinner."

Equal Participation: Lastly, make sure all people has an identical possibility to take part. This method all of us gets a threat to speak, make contributions to the talk, and percent their mind and feelings. It may be useful to designate a assembly leader to guide the communicate and make certain every person's voice is heard.

Example: If your more youthful son is quiet at some level inside the meeting, the chief may additionally say, "We have now not heard from you but, should you want to proportion your mind on this?"

These floor guidelines are simply an area to start. Depending in your own family's unique dynamics, you could need to add additional policies. The critical trouble is that every one regulations are agreed upon by way of the use of all people and enforced continuously in the course of every assembly. This will help ensure that your circle of relatives meetings are efficient, respectful, and useful for absolutely everyone concerned. In the subsequent section, we can talk the essential characteristic of hassle-fixing during family meetings.

Here are some more floor rules that is probably beneficial to your family conferences:

Be Honest, But Kind: Honesty is crucial in circle of relatives meetings because it enables in identifying troubles and springing up with powerful answers. However, honesty have to not be used as an excuse to be endorse or hurtful. Encourage all of us to explicit themselves honestly but kindly.

Example: Instead of pronouncing, "Your room is constantly a multitude, it's far disgusting," try announcing, "I observed that it is difficult so one can hold your room tidy. Maybe we are capable of come up with a gadget together that makes it lots less hard for you."

Confidentiality: What's mentioned in the circle of relatives assembly want to stay in the circle of relatives, until it's far some component that desires to be shared for protection or fitness motives. This rule encourages openness and take delivery of as real with.

Example: If your elder daughter shares her struggles with a pal at college, this statistics have to not be shared outside of the circle of relatives with out her consent.

No Electronics: To ensure that everybody is gift and not distracted, it's miles a top notch idea to have a rule approximately no electronics in the course of the meeting, except they're vital for the speak or time table.

Example: Everyone leaves their telephones, tablets, or superb digital gadgets in every one of a kind room in the path of the meeting.

Start and End on Time: Respect everybody's time with the resource of beginning and completing the meeting as scheduled.

This encourages punctuality and suggests that everybody's time is valued.

Example: If the assembly is scheduled to start at 7:00 PM, ensure that it starts at that element, no matter whether or no longer surely everyone is present. This might encourage punctuality in destiny meetings.

Positivity Rule: Begin and give up every meeting on a high-quality be conscious. This may be sharing some aspect properly that passed off at some degree in the week or expressing appreciation for each wonderful.

Example: Start the assembly with the resource of every member sharing a few aspect specific that passed off to them within the week. Similarly, give up the assembly via the use of pronouncing a few thing you recognize approximately everybody present.

Agree to Disagree: In any employer dialogue, it's far everyday for disagreements to stand up. The 'comply with disagree' rule permits remind all and sundry that it's miles ok to have exclusive reviews, and the aim isn't to win an trouble, but to find out a answer that works for the circle of relatives.

Example: If there may be a heated war of words on whether or no longer to have a family tour or not, you can say, "It seems like we've were given exquisite evaluations in this depend, and that is ok. Let's try to find out a answer that considers absolutely everyone's factor of view."

Remember, the purpose is to create an environment of recognize, open conversation, and cooperation. These recommendations have to be designed to assist that goal and may be changed as preferred to suit your family's precise desires.

Making Meetings Positive and Productive

Family meetings are a important aspect of the own family planning blueprint due to the truth they offer the platform for everyday open discussions, improvement test-ins, trouble-fixing, and celebrations of fulfillment. However, for the own family assembly to be truly effective, it's far crucial to preserve the surroundings high-quality and the conversations green. Here's how you can accomplish this:

Focus on Solutions, Not Blame

In a own family assembly, troubles will continually rise up. When they do, it's far essential that the dialogue focuses on finding a solution instead of blaming a person. Casting blame can create a horrific environment and discourage open conversation. Instead, view problems as something that the family as an entire desires to treatment.

For example, if one little one is continuously failing to complete their chores, the communication need to recognition on information why this is going on and what can be finished to assist in desire to blaming the child for now not doing their detail.

Ensure Everyone Has a Voice

Every family member need to enjoy heard and valued in a family meeting. Make effective definitely every body has an opportunity to talk and that their opinions are listened to and revered, even the more youthful individuals of the circle of relatives. It may be useful to introduce a 'speaking stick' or some distinctive token that someone holds when it is their turn to talk to make certain this.

For instance, while discussing in which to move on a family excursion, ensure simply anyone has a chance to specific their possibilities and ideas. This no longer best makes every person experience worried but also can bring about discovering options you hadn't thought of.

Recognize and Celebrate Achievements

Part of maintaining the meeting outstanding is taking time to recognize and feature amusing achievements, irrespective of how small. This can boom morale and encourage family individuals to hold walking inside the path in their dreams. Always leave some time in each meeting for a round of applause for the week's achievements.

For instance, if a member of the family reached a private purpose or made large improvement on their a part of the circle of relatives plan, take a second to renowned this and feature a laugh it.

Keep the Atmosphere Light

Remember, family meetings need to now not experience like a chore or a proper corporation assembly. Keep the surroundings moderate and first-rate to encourage participation. You can begin with a spherical of jokes, or a quick, amusing own family activity. This can make circle of relatives conferences something all and sundry appears ahead to in place of an obligation.

In conclusion, with the useful resource of that specialize in answers, making sure every body has a voice, celebrating achievements, and keeping the atmosphere slight, your circle of relatives conferences can be every first-rate and green. This will allow your circle of relatives to work together successfully in the route of the common desires you've got set to your family making plans blueprint.

As we have got were given cited, own family conferences characteristic the precept platform to check development, cope with boundaries, and hold alignment at the family's overarching goals. The Family Plan, with its Ultimate Goal, sub-desires, and private goals, offers the framework for the ones discussions. While later chapters will delve deeper into the introduction of person blueprints and the overall Family Plan Blueprint, allow's speak how those plans can be blanketed into your circle of relatives conferences.

Reviewing Progress

Each circle of relatives meeting want to include a examine of development made inside the route of the Family Plan and man or woman blueprints. Family people can percent updates on their private desires, sub-desires, and obligations they had been working on. Celebrate any achievements, irrespective of how small they'll appear. This not only motivates human beings however additionally shows how every body's efforts are contributing to the family's everyday purpose.

For instance, if one family member's private motive changed into to decorate their bodily fitness, and they efficiently caught to their exercising regular for the week, it's a development well really worth celebrating.

Addressing Obstacles

Challenges and obstacles are element and parcel of any purpose-putting method. Family meetings are an fantastic opportunity to together deal with those troubles. When a member of the family faces a venture in their direction towards their non-public goals, they could percentage it in the course of the assembly. The family, as a collective unit, can brainstorm and provide manual to overcome the hurdle.

Suppose a member of the family is struggling to hold cash as that they'd deliberate. This issue can be stated all through the assembly, and others can endorse answers or strategies that helped them in similar conditions.

Adjusting and Refining the Plan

As your family progresses towards its dreams, you can discover that some elements of your plan need to be adjusted. Family meetings provide a platform to talk approximately the ones capability modifications. Perhaps a private aim wants to be recalibrated or a wonderful method is needed for a sub-goal.

For example, if a member of the family had set a intention to examine a ebook each week but reveals this to be unrealistic with their current-day time table, they might regulate it to analyzing a ebook each weeks as an alternative.

Bringing the Blueprint to Life

The most critical component of those meetings is how they assist to hold the family's blueprint to life. Each talk, choice, and celebration enables to construct and solidify the stairs for your plan, turning the blueprint from a static record right right into a dwelling, respiration approach for achieving your circle of relatives's shared imaginative and prescient.

In forestall, imposing the Family Plan into your family meetings may be an incredibly powerful approach for preserving without a doubt everyone aligned, stimulated, and prepared to overcome any limitations inside the manner of your dreams. As we delve deeper into the specifics of creating person blueprints and the general Family Plan Blueprint within the later chapters, the ones meetings becomes even extra vital to your family's achievement.

Dealing with Setbacks

Setbacks and demanding situations are an inevitable part of any journey within the course of a large purpose. These moments may be particularly tough after they affect the whole circle of relatives or whilst character traumatic situations begin to impact the own family's collective progress. However, those hurdles, while irritating, moreover may be an opportunity for boom and resilience.

Emphasizing Resilience

Resilience is the functionality to get better from adversity and keep a amazing outlook no matter the difficulties we come upon. It's a useful outstanding to foster inside your own family unit. During your own family conferences, give a lift to the idea that setbacks are quick and that every challenge gives a hazard to analyze and increase.

For instance, if a member of the family has struggled to satisfy their private goal for the week, encourage them to mirror on what they may do in any other case and the manner they may modify their technique. Remember, the purpose proper right here isn't to stay on the failure but to focus on the direction forward.

Problem-Solving Together

A big gain of having a set up own family assembly is that it offers a platform to collaboratively cope with issues. Encourage circle of relatives members to deliver their challenges to the table, and method those issues as a collective trouble-fixing exercise. This not best allows in finding solutions however additionally builds a experience of concord and shared duty.

Imagine, for instance, the family is collectively looking to reduce family costs, and they may be no longer hitting their goal. This setback may be mentioned in the assembly, and anyone can share mind and techniques to hold down prices. The collective brainstorming would probably motive progressive answers that one person might not have idea of on their private.

The Power of Family Unity

One of the maximum sturdy equipment your circle of relatives has in dealing with setbacks is the power of your concord. The family's collective guide and reassurance can assist people navigate their non-public problems, and joint challenges may be triumph over through way of leveraging each person's particular strengths.

Remind every family member that they may be not on my own in their struggles and that the family, as a unit, is there to assist them. Similarly, at the same time as the family faces a shared task, take into account that really each person brings a completely unique mind-set and set of skills to the desk which can make a contribution to the solution.

In give up, setbacks have to now not be seen as insurmountable barriers, however as an opportunity opportunities for studying, growth, and strengthening the bond inner your family. By emphasizing resilience, fostering collective trouble-solving, and harnessing the energy of your circle of relatives's cohesion, you may navigate these annoying conditions and maintain transferring toward your desires.

Evolving the Family Meetings

Just like your circle of relatives dreams and the human beings inside the own family, your family conferences too will evolve over time. This evolution may be driven via manner of different factors - accomplishing old desires, setting new ones, changes in circle of relatives instances, or sincerely the developing maturity and converting dynamics of the circle of relatives unit.

For example, as your circle of relatives gets greater conversant in the circle of relatives assembly shape, you can find out the conferences turning into more streamlined and green. Initially, you may probably spend numerous time explaining necessities, placing ground rules, and addressing resistance. But over time, those become 2d nature, permitting you to spend more time on the middle communicate factors collectively with development updates, problem-fixing, and intention-placing.

Achieving a massive family purpose can also bring about evolution for your own family conferences. With the accomplishment of a massive reason, it is time to set new ones. This might likely shift the focus of your meetings as you start to break down those new desires and chart out the roadmap to build up them.

Similarly, modifications in family occasions, in conjunction with a member beginning a cutting-edge faculty or undertaking, can shift the point of interest of your conferences. These modifications can result in new traumatic situations and dreams, requiring adjustments within the assembly shape or the circle of relatives plan.

In give up, it's miles critical to consider that your own family meetings are not set in stone. They are dynamic, much like your own family, and that they need to adapt to serve the converting dreams of your family's adventure toward its desires.

As we end Chapter three, we are hoping which you're starting to see how family conferences can end up a effective tool to your circle of relatives planning efforts. However, to make the ones conferences, and surely, the complete family making plans manner sincerely effective, there may be one more crucial detail we want to hobby on - communique.

Chapter 4: The Importance Of Communication

In our adventure to create an effective Family Plan, we cannot forget about the significance of 1 essential detail – conversation. It's the lifeblood of any a success courting, and families aren't any exception. This bankruptcy will shine a spotlight at the location of communique in circle of relatives planning. We will speak its significance, come to be aware of not unusual barriers, and offer strategies to beautify it internal your own family.

Imagine looking for to play a group recreation wherein no one communicates. The game enthusiasts are all gifted, all of them want to win, but no person is coordinating, nobody is privy to what the others are planning, and anybody is performing based mostly on assumptions or their very personal person know-how of the sport. Chances are, that group would possibly no longer win many video video games.

Family planning, like that group game, requires communique. It's how we express our thoughts, percent our mind, and understand each specific. It's how we collect bridges of information and empathy. In the context of a own family plan, communique serves numerous essential roles:

Fostering Understanding: Clear and open communication lets in circle of relatives people understand every other higher. We all have unique mind, feelings, and perspectives. Expressing the ones correctly can sell a deeper understanding and mutual admire.

Aligning Goals: Every member of the family might have considered one of a kind private dreams. Communication aids in aligning those character dreams with the overarching circle of relatives dreams, making sure everyone is going for walks within the route of a shared cause.

Promoting Cooperation: Effective communication complements cooperation. When family individuals can articulate their mind, wishes, and expectancies, it makes it much less tough for clearly all of us to art work together.

In the following sections, we are capable of delve deeper into how we are able to nurture effective conversation inner our families, overcome common barriers, and use communication as a device to beautify our circle of relatives making plans efforts.

Barriers to Effective Communication

While we understand the important characteristic communication plays in our family making plans, it's far similarly critical to understand that powerful verbal exchange would possibly now not come smooth. There can be numerous limitations that stand within the manner, making conversations tough and even counterproductive. Let's take a more in-depth have a look at some commonplace boundaries and the way they may prevent powerful conversation in a own family putting:

Misunderstandings: We've all been there - you're pronouncing one detail, and the opportunity man or woman hears some issue in reality first-rate. Misunderstandings are a commonplace conversation barrier. They can arise because of versions in belief, interpretation, or maybe easy mishearing. Misunderstandings can bring about confusion and discord, obstructing the improvement towards our own family dreams.

Assumptions: Assumptions also can impede powerful communique. We frequently anticipate that we recognize what the alternative character technique or that they understand us, without confirming our expertise. These assumptions can reason large communication gaps, leaving room for errors and causing frustration.

Lack of Listening Skills: Effective communication is as a fantastic deal about speakme as it's far approximately listening. Yet, listening is a potential that often receives ignored. We're often so centered on what we want to say subsequent that we do not absolutely soak up what the opportunity character is saying. This loss of active listening can result in misunderstandings and avoid powerful conversation.

Emotional Barriers: Emotional boundaries which includes anger, frustration, or resentment can significantly avert conversation. When feelings run immoderate, they may coloration our perceptions and interpretations, making it hard to talk efficiently.

Differing Communication Styles: Every person has a totally specific communication fashion. Some people is probably more direct, at the identical time as others might be extra roundabout. Some can also additionally pick to specific themselves thru terms, whilst others may also moreover rely greater on non-verbal cues. These differences in verbal exchange patterns can sometimes emerge as a barrier to effective conversation.

By spotting those obstacles, we're able to take steps to address them, paving the manner for additonal open, knowledge, and effective communication interior our households. In the following sections, we're able to find out techniques and strategies to overcome those limitations and decorate our conversation skills.

Strategies for Effective Communication

Effective verbal exchange is fundamental to a a achievement own family plan. It permits us to understand every different, align our efforts toward our commonplace dreams, and treatment troubles effectively. In moderate of the limitations we mentioned within the preceding section, proper here are some effective techniques to decorate conversation within your own family:

Active Listening: This is the primary and probably most crucial technique for boosting verbal exchange. Active listening includes no longer surely being attentive to what the possibility person is pronouncing, however sincerely knowledge their message and mindset. It consists of supplying feedback, asking clarifying questions, and avoiding distractions whilst listening. Remember, at the equal time as you are actively listening, you are signaling to the opposite character that their perspective is valued.

Clear and Concise Expression: To keep away from misunderstandings, it is important to explicit ourselves truly and concisely. This involves being specific about what we need or want, offering suitable enough context, and warding off vague or ambiguous language. Keep your messages straightforward and to the aspect, and make certain that your tone and frame language align together with your terms.

Empathetic Responses: Empathy involves setting your self in someone else's shoes and expertise their emotions. Responding with empathy can help to assemble bear in mind, validate the alternative individual's emotions, and pave the way for more open and honest conversation. It includes acknowledging their emotions and showing genuine situation for his or her desires and tales.

Nonverbal Communication: Remember, communication isn't pretty a remarkable deal phrases. Facial expressions, eye touch, body language, and tone of voice also can communicate lots approximately how we are feeling. Be aware of your non-public nonverbal cues and learn how to study those of others as well.

Ask for Clarification: If you are unsure approximately what a person is attempting to speak, do no longer hesitate to invite for clarification. This can assist prevent misunderstandings and indicates which you're actively engaged in the communication and fee their input.

Open-mindedness: Lastly, effective communication calls for an open mind. Be open to the mind and opinions of others, even though they vary out of your very very personal. This allows foster an environment wherein everyone feels heard and revered, encouraging extra open and sincere verbal exchange.

By implementing these strategies, we are able to assist facilitate greater effective conversation within our families, number one to a greater harmonious and powerful circle of relatives making plans approach.

Role of Communication in Conflict Resolution

Effective communication is not quite a whole lot expressing ourselves and records others, however it is also a critical tool for resolving conflicts. It's natural for disagreements to upward thrust up inner a circle of relatives, however how we manipulate those disagreements can significantly have an effect at the harmony and harmony within the family unit. Let's discover how we are capable of leverage communication skills to remedy disputes effectively.

Open Dialogue: The first step to war resolution is putting in place a speak approximately the problem handy. It's critical to create a solid area wherein each party feels cushty expressing their viewpoints without fear of judgment or retaliation.

Active Listening: As mentioned in advance, energetic listening is a essential verbal exchange talent. In the context of struggle choice, it permits ensure that everyone's viewpoints are understood and brought into consideration. Active listening consists of no longer sincerely hearing, but in reality data and validating the alternative individual's mindset.

Use "I" Statements: Expressing our feelings and worries the usage of "I" statements can help to prevent defensive responses. For instance, in choice to announcing, "You in no way assist with the chores," strive announcing, "I revel in beaten as soon as I need to cope with all of the chores on my own." This approach makes a speciality of your feelings in area of blaming or criticizing the opportunity man or woman.

Seek to Understand, Then to be Understood: Before putting forth your angle, ensure that you completely recognize the alternative man or woman's attitude. This no longer excellent suggests appreciate for his or her emotions and reviews, however can also assist you communicate your very very own angle in a way that they'll understand and accumulate.

Focus on the Issue, Not the Person: During conflicts, it is critical to interest on the trouble available and no longer inn to private attacks. Avoid blaming, criticizing or making hurtful remarks. Instead, attention at the problem and the manner it could be resolved.

Use Calm and Respectful Tone: The manner we are pronouncing subjects regularly includes greater weight than the terms we use. Even in a few unspecified time within the destiny of disagreements, hold a non violent and respectful tone. This can help prevent the scenario from escalating and maintains the point of interest on resolving the hassle.

Seek Win-Win Solutions: The intention of battle decision need to not be to 'win' the argument, however to discover an answer this is appropriate to everybody. This often calls for compromise and indicates that everyone's dreams and feelings are valued.

Effective verbal exchange is a beneficial tool in conflict decision. By the use of the ones techniques, we are in a position to turn potentially unfavorable conflicts into opportunities for facts, boom, and in addition bonding in the circle of relatives. The secret is to preserve recognize and information for each exclusive's viewpoints, even within the face of conflict of words.

Communication and Goal Setting

Just as effective communication is vital in battle choice, it's far similarly vital in the technique of setting and undertaking own family goals. Clear, consistent, and open communique guarantees anybody is at the identical net page and contributes in the direction of conducting the collective goals.

Transparency in Goal Setting: When setting own family dreams, it's far important that each one own family contributors have a clear understanding of what those goals are. This consists of understanding why the ones desires had been chosen, how they gain the own family, and what the plan is to gain them. This degree of transparency can be completed through open and sincere verbal exchange.

Regular Updates and Progress Reports: Regular verbal exchange approximately the progress of the goals is crucial to preserve everyone involved and inspired. This does no longer advocate surely sharing the successes, however also the demanding situations encountered along the way. Such updates may be shared inside the route of the own family conferences we cited inside the preceding chapter.

Clarity of Roles and Responsibilities: Every family member has a position to play in assignment the family goals. These roles and the corresponding duties should be really communicated to avoid misunderstandings and make sure each person is privy to what is predicted of them.

Feedback and Adjustments: The gadget of operating closer to goals is dynamic, no longer static. There might be times while modifications want to be made. Whether it's a exchange in method, department of duties, or maybe re-comparing the desires themselves, those adjustments have to be communicated honestly to all own family individuals.

Celebrating Successes Together: Just as demanding conditions have to be communicated, so must successes. Whether it is a small milestone or the fulfillment of a large goal, these moments must be celebrated collectively. Not satisfactory does this act as a morale booster, however it additionally strengthens the bond in the family.

Effective communique office work the spine of motive setting and achievement in the family. When every family member is aware of the goals, is aware of their thing in reaching them, and is saved up to date about the progress, it fosters a experience of brotherly love, reason, and collective achievement. Remember, the system of project the goal may be simply as vital because of the reality the intention itself. It's this adventure wherein useful instructions are positioned, bonds are bolstered, and memories are made.

Communication, as we've got were given seen, is the lifeblood of powerful family planning. It bridges statistics, fosters cooperation, and lets in us to navigate conflict, making it a key thing of successful purpose setting and fulfillment. From truely expressing expectations to actively listening and providing empathetic responses, each of these elements of conversation plays a critical characteristic in shaping the own family's course and development inside the path of their desires.

Just as inside the context of our individual lives, within the circle of relatives placing too, limitations are inevitable. However, it is through open and respectful communique that we turns into privy to, cope with, and overcome those boundaries, turning them into stepping stones in the direction of our collective goals. It's moreover through this manner that we enhance our relationships with every one of a kind, developing an environment it isn't honestly purpose-orientated, however additionally supportive and nurturing.

As we near this financial disaster, undergo in thoughts that like some exceptional competencies, conversation too requires normal exercising and refinement. Each communique, each assembly is an opportunity to higher our communication and consequently, our journey closer to our goals.

Having tested the function of verbal exchange in circle of relatives making plans, we are now higher ready to delve into the realistic elements of crafting your Family Plan. In the subsequent economic spoil, we're capable of explore the way to mix all of the factors we've mentioned to date—desires, blueprints, obligations, meetings, and verbal exchange—into an actionable, powerful Family Plan. This may be a palms-on bankruptcy, guiding you step-thru-step via growing your very very very own Family Plan that is precise on your circle of relatives's dreams and conditions. So, let's roll up our sleeves and get geared up to place our information into motion!

Chapter 5: Creating The Family Vision

Creating the Family Vision highlights the power of shared goals and the unifying impact of a collective vision. This is a pivotal financial disaster, a a laugh and appealing turning element in our adventure. This is in which we initiate the exciting manner of visually taking pics your circle of relatives's aspirations on a vision board, a tangible reflected photo of your shared dreams and desires. This vision board isn't truely an inspirational piece; it's a realistic device on the way to be applied in the following chapters. It will function a springboard for figuring out character and circle of relatives goals, if you want to be contrary engineered into sub-dreams, each day, and weekly responsibilities. This method lets in to ground your circle of relatives's imaginative and prescient into tangible, capability steps that lead inside the path of its focus.

In this bankruptcy, we're able to find out the importance of a shared family vision and why it's miles critical on your circle of relatives's journey. We are not really human beings residing under the same roof, however a fixed running towards not unusual goals. This collective imaginative and prescient will function a beacon, guiding your alternatives, inspiring anyone in the own family, and fostering a enjoy of organization spirit. A well-defined own family vision has the strength to inspire, to manual us in instances of uncertainty, and to reinforce our remedy even as we are going via annoying conditions.

A own family vision is extra than only a set of person aspirations. It is a unifying stress, an agreed-upon excursion spot that every one people of the family are excited to obtain. The journey closer to undertaking this shared vision can convey a own family nearer, promoting a deeper expertise of every other and fostering an environment of mutual apprehend and collaboration. This shared vision will manual your own family's decisions, allowing you to navigate stressful conditions and possibilities with a clean cause and route.

At this juncture, it is important to endure in thoughts that the own family imaginative and prescient is a mixture of all of the goals and aspirations of its people. In the following section, we are able to talk a a laugh and creative approach to taking photos the ones desires and aspirations: the creation of a Family Vision Board. This shared interest isn't great a effective device for visualisation, however additionally a first-rate possibility for own family bonding.

I'm thrilled to guide you via one of the most thrilling factors of our adventure: developing your Family Vision Board. This fingers-on, interactive experience serves as a amusing and tangible expression of your collective aspirations.

Creating a Family Vision Board

Before we dive into the approach, permit's make certain you have got the whole thing desired for this family hobby. You'll want one or huge white poster forums - these are successfully to be had in grocery or administrative center deliver stores. Get some colourful non-poisonous markers or a few different writing system you pick. And of course, keep in mind to supply your favourite circle of relatives snacks and refreshments! Incorporating acquainted, fun factors into your Family Meeting lets in create outstanding establishments and encourages keen participation.

Once your substances are collected, it is time to name the own family assembly. A institution textual content, a word at the fridge, or a simple verbal announcement can art work. The intention is to ensure absolutely everyone is aware about the meeting and might make it. Then, it's time to collect throughout the table and dive into the amusing!

Start the meeting with a quick clarification of why you're all here: to create a shared Family Vision Board. This is a visual illustration of your family's dreams and aspirations, a device with a view to guide you in the direction of your collective dreams.

Now, location the clean poster board within the center of the desk. Draw a large circle in the middle of the board. This circle is your family's coronary heart, the middle of your shared vision. Have each person take turns writing what they take delivery of as genuine with the own family desires are, or what they would like to be proper approximately the circle of relatives in the destiny. Encourage absolutely everyone to talk their thoughts freely - there aren't any wrong answers in this exercise, fine actual expressions of your circle of relatives's shared desires.

Once everybody has had a chance to make contributions to the fundamental circle, it's time to boom. Outside of this circle, have every family member write smaller desires or thoughts that make a contribution to achieving the matters written within the center. Encourage a lively communicate and exchange of mind as every member of the family affords to the board.

Remember, that is your own family's vision. It's unique, similar to each one in all you. Enjoy this revolutionary technique, have a laugh, and hold an open mind. The creation of your Family Vision Board isn't always just an crucial step within the path of attaining your goals; it's far a celebration of your shared desires and the strength of your family bond.

Moving immediately to the subsequent phase of our adventure, allow's communicate approximately how we're capable of combine this shared vision into our ordinary lives.

Integrating the Family Vision into Daily Life

A imaginative and prescient this is out of sight is frequently out of thoughts. To maintain your own family vision alive and applicable, make it part of your each day lifestyles. Display the Family Vision Board prominently in a common region of your property wherein anyone can see it. It can be the kitchen, the dwelling room, or another location that your family regularly gathers. Seeing it each day will function a ordinary reminder of your shared goals and aspirations.

Refer to the Family Vision Board at some point of your own family conferences. It serves as a seen cue that allows align your own family discussions and choice-making with the shared vision. It moreover offers a tangible diploma of your improvement, as you examine your dreams and desires come to existence over the years.

Revisit your Family Vision Board periodically. Review the desires and goals inscribed on it. Reflect at the improvement you have made. Make updates as vital to reflect changing conditions or new aspirations. Remember, this imaginative and prescient board is a residing report, evolving along with your own family.

As a sneak peek into the subsequent Family Meeting, we are going to be embarking on a comparable workout - growing person Vision

Boards. While the Family Vision Board indicates our collective goals, the individual Vision Boards will cater to personal dreams and aspirations. They may not apprehend it however, but those man or woman forums are a important step within the path of the awesome Blueprint introduction in the upcoming conferences. With each step, you are not best bringing your family closer collectively, however moreover placing the extent for each member to map out their route to achievement. Stay tuned, and keep to encompass this interesting adventure of increase and accomplishment!

Chapter 6: Setting Individual Goals

As we development towards the subsequent exciting family assembly, wherein every member can be developing their personal vision board, allow's take a pause to apprehend some key aspects of person purpose setting.

Just as a own family vision unifies a family toward shared dreams, individual goals serve a crucial characteristic in personal increase and improvement. They provide a sense of path, instill reason, and inspire movements. More importantly, those private dreams aren't standalone pastimes. They feed into, and frequently boost up, the adventure inside the course of our collective circle of relatives imaginative and prescient. Individual goals are like the right threads in a tapestry, each contributing to the beautiful format that is your circle of relatives imaginative and prescient.

Understanding Personal Aspirations

Before putting desires, it's far crucial to delve into one's non-public aspirations. To find out those, a deeper expertise of one's passions, interests, and goals is needed. We all have a unique internal compass guided with the aid of the usage of using our aspirations. Reflecting on questions like 'What am I enthusiastic about?', 'What would I need to benefit in a specific time body?', 'What brings me pleasure?' can display insights about one's aspirations. These function fertile ground from which desires can be cultivated.

Setting Age-Appropriate Goals

As we set person dreams, it's miles critical to ensure they will be age-appropriate. For more younger circle of relatives contributors, goals may be as simple as enhancing a capability, taking up a cutting-edge-day interest, or accomplishing higher grades in a selected situation. Teenagers may reputation on university schooling, gaining art work enjoy, or non-public increase goals. Adults need to set dreams around career progression, economic planning, health, and personal improvement. The beauty of this system is that every body's goals, irrespective of how severa, make contributions to the tapestry of the circle of relatives's collective vision. The key right right right here is to ensure every member of the family, from the youngest to the oldest, has their non-public pursuits mentioned and respected.

Creating Personal Vision Boards

We're now organized to embark at the a laugh and enriching workout of creating non-public imaginative and prescient boards. Just like we did in the previous bankruptcy for the own family vision board, this manner calls for a similar accumulating, an open and inclusive circle of relatives assembly. We will provide each member of the family with their canvas to creatively visualize their individual desires and aspirations.

Materials Needed: Again, acquire your materials in advance - a massive poster board for every family member, a set of colorful non-poisonous markers, and an collection of magazines, newspapers, or printouts for pics and phrases that may be pasted at the forums. Don't forget about about the scissors and glue!

Getting Started: Plan and alert the circle of relatives for the next circle of relatives meeting. At the meeting, gather the own family round a table, making sure all of us has their sources. Put their clean boards inside the front of them. Kickstart the consultation through way of reminding certainly all of us that the ones personal vision forums will function visual reminders of their person dreams, as a way to, in flip, contribute to the overall family imaginative and prescient.

Creating the Vision Board: Have all of us draw a massive circle inside the middle of their board. They must write their maximum critical goals or aspirations proper here, those who align maximum carefully with their private values and goals. Encourage them to consider what they would like to obtain or what they want to be real about themselves in the destiny.

Next, have them jot down smaller dreams or steps throughout the critical circle on the way to make a contribution to venture the primary dreams. They can add photos and phrases from the magazines, newspapers, or printouts that constitute those dreams or the feeling they companion with carrying out them. These forums need to be colourful, lively, and provoking!

Using the Vision Board: Once the vision boards are entire, discuss how they will be used to inspire and inspire. They need to be located someplace every body will see them every day. This will feature a everyday reminder of what they will be working towards.

Having person desires is an empowering step inside the direction of private boom. Yet, the ones desires must align with the family imaginative and prescient to create a unified course in the direction of shared success. As you wrap up the Personal Vision Board exercise to your circle of relatives meeting, provoke a verbal exchange all through the alignment of private objectives together collectively with your collective aspirations.

Encourage every member of the family to percentage their vision board and deliver an purpose of the dreams they've got written down. This is an possibility for others to understand every person's individual aspirations higher and observe how the ones align with the family's broader vision. As actually all people stocks, try to perceive commonplace topics or complementary dreams that tie into the own family's collective dreams. This workout isn't to scrutinize or critique, but as an alternative to have a good time anybody's desires and word how they make a contribution to the circle of relatives's shared imaginative and prescient.

In the ones discussions, enhance the concept that goals are not set in stone; they are dynamic and might alternate as people expand and occasions shift. Encourage own family participants to revisit their non-public imaginative and prescient forums frequently, assessing their relevance and realism. Are the goals but exciting and extensive to them? Do they want to be adjusted to stay in keeping with converting non-public aspirations or circle of relatives situations?

Creating a everyday time table for revisiting and adjusting the ones dreams may be beneficial. Perhaps this will be an schedule object to your monthly family conferences? Adjusting dreams does now not suggest failure; instead, it's miles a signal of boom, adaptability, and practical making plans.

This everyday revisiting and adjusting not splendid maintains man or woman dreams sparkling and applicable, but it moreover fosters non-stop talk spherical non-public development and own family development. Remember, the journey in your desires is simply as essential because of the truth the destination, and preserving the verbal exchange going is a essential a part of that adventure.

In this exciting financial ruin, we've were given not best understood the significance of individual goals, however we have moreover taken a massive step within the route of growing a harmonious route for collective own family fulfillment. By know-how private aspirations and aligning them with the own family vision, we've were given painted a colourful tapestry of goals and ambitions, each character and shared.

We found out a manner to craft Personal Vision Boards and the manner the ones characteristic colourful representations of our individual goals. Through growing those forums, we've got allowed all and sundry to articulate their dreams and aspirations without a doubt.

Chapter 7: From Goals To Plans- Creating A Personal Blueprint

In this pivotal bankruptcy, we are transitioning from visions to actions. This phase of the adventure calls for a few other own family meeting, wherein each member will embark at the task of opposite-engineering their personal goals from their imaginative and prescient boards. The purpose? To convert those aspirations into actionable steps or obligations, thereby forming the foundation in their Personal Blueprint. This Personal Blueprint is more than first-class a roadmap—it's far an in depth guide that takes every reason and breaks it down into conceivable milestones.

Keep in mind, this blueprint isn't always a rigid shape. Rather, it's far a dynamic record that evolves with you and your own family, adapting for your development, and gaining knowledge of over the years. It serves as your guiding slight, illuminating the direction to private and circle of relatives achievement. So, gather your circle of relatives, convey your vision forums, and get equipped to convert your collective desires into an actionable truth, one step at a time.

Understanding the Personal Blueprint.

This chapter will delve into the approach of creating a non-public blueprint, an essential a part of your family planning journey. The Personal Blueprint isn't always similar to your vision board in its degree of element and practical utility. If your vision board is the holiday spot, then your Personal Blueprint is the step-thru-step manual on the manner to get there.

While the imaginative and prescient board captures your overarching goals and aspirations, your Personal Blueprint takes every of these dreams and breaks them down into concrete steps, smaller duties, and actionable timelines. It serves as your private roadmap, guiding you in your journey inside the route of attaining your character desires.

The Personal Blueprint is a important device for success as it gives form in your dreams, supplying a tangible plan that could manual your every day actions. By mapping out your adventure and putting clean, doable milestones, your blueprint permits you stay focused and stimulated. It allows to bridge the distance amongst wherein you are now and in which you aspire to be.

Moreover, the device of making a Personal Blueprint permits you to recognize your goals at a deeper diploma, highlighting what is required to acquire them. By detailing the movements and belongings wanted, it fosters a revel in of responsibility, encouraging you to take ownership of your adventure.

In the following sections, we will guide you at the manner to create this effective tool and use it to navigate your course to personal and family success.

Reverse Engineering Your Goals

The transformation of goals into actionable steps is in which actual improvement starts. The technique of contrary engineering your dreams will bring about your Personal Blueprint. It's a seen and sensible manual that will help you navigate your manner to reaching your desires.

Reference yet again to Chapter 2 for a visual example of a Blueprint as wanted, but let's run through every other example- this time try to write out your own non-public goals if you haven't already!

Make wonderful you have a massive piece of paper or a pocket ebook, and a pen available.

Start by means of manner of writing down one of the important goals from the center of your imaginative and prescient board inside the pinnacle proper nook of your paper. Draw a box spherical this essential cause. This most important goal is your last goal, your dream to be achieved.

Underneath your critical goal, listing out the huge steps you want to take to attain this motive, the sub-goals. Draw a container round every sub-goal. In the field, beneath the call of each sub-aim, write down some subjects which you would really like to be actual as soon as you've got executed this sub-reason. For example, if your sub-purpose is "Learn to play the guitar," you can want that "I can play 3 entire songs," or "I can play with out looking at the strings."

Now, take each sub-goal and preserve in mind smaller steps or movements wanted to perform it. Write those moves to the left of every sub-purpose, growing a type of go with the flow from right to left to your paper. Draw a box round every motion and listing the topics that need to be completed or the conditions that want to be met for this movement to be finished. For instance, for the motion "Sign up for guitar lessons," you will in all likelihood write, "Research nearby track schools," or "Budget for lesson expenses."

Look again at some point of your blueprint and select out each day or weekly duties from the actions needed to begin moving in the direction of completing the steps and overarching goals. For instance, placing aside 15 minutes every day for on line research on tune colleges is probably a every day task.

Take the ones each day and weekly responsibilities and upload them into your day planner or virtual calendar. This will make certain you are actively working in the direction of your dreams every day. It might also additionally help you visualize your progress and preserve momentum.

This Personal Blueprint is a dwelling record. It will evolve as you're making development, face stressful situations, and look at extra approximately your dreams and the stairs to achieve them. Remember to revisit it frequently, alter as wanted, and feature a laugh every leap forward.

The Role of Flexibility in Your Blueprint

In this adventure of attaining our dreams and goals, there is one steady—exchange. As John Lennon famously sang, "Life is what occurs to you whilst you're busy making other plans." We want to in reality receive and include the inherent unpredictability of life. It is vital to bear in mind that your Personal Blueprint is a manual, a roadmap—it isn't always set in stone.

Think of your blueprint as a route on a GPS device. It affords a smooth path from trouble A to factor B, but now and again, you could come across sudden site visitors, road closures, or you might clearly determine to take a scenic detour. Similarly, existence will present sudden stressful conditions, possibilities, and analyzing experiences which could necessitate a trade for your plan. The secret is flexibility.

It's flawlessly appropriate, and frequently vital, to modify your obligations and movements on your blueprint as activities alternate. You might also moreover apprehend that a selected step isn't as relevant anymore, or that a one-of-a-kind method might be greater powerful. You can also moreover discover new pursuits or passions which have an impact for your important dreams.

As you develop and evolve, so will your goals and the stairs to obtain them. It's a dynamic technique. Therefore, be open to revising your blueprint as required. Don't understand the ones adjustments as setbacks, however as a ordinary a part of the approach. The capability to comply and evolve your plan within the face of exchange is a electricity, not a prone factor.

Remember, the final purpose of your blueprint is to help you attain your goals in a way that aligns with your existence and values. It's now not a inflexible rulebook, however a flexible manual designed to navigate you in the direction of your goals. The success of your journey is not decided thru a proper away line, but by means of your resilience and capability to comply to existence's ebb and go along with the drift.

Regular Review and Celebration of Progress

Maintaining momentum on our course to success is essential, and key practices useful aid in this: everyday have a look at and birthday celebration of improvement.

Consider scheduling a consistent time, probable weekly or monthly, to test your Personal Blueprint. This is a hazard to assess your development, regulate your obligations and moves if wished, and realign your consciousness. This habitual maintains your desires glowing on your thoughts and reinforces your willpower to sporting out them.

Equally critical is the birthday party of development, regardless of how small. Every leap ahead, every container you take a look at off to your blueprint, is a victory nicely worth celebrating. These celebrations, be they big or small, function powerful motivation, enhancing your momentum. They remind you which you're capable of development and growth, fuelling your adventure closer to your vital goal. Celebrating development fosters a powerful mindset and maintains the adventure fun and pleasant.

Remember, the journey to benefit our goals isn't a sprint however a marathon. Regular opinions and celebrations of improvement are the milestones that preserve us going, make the journey fun, and convey us towards our dreams.

The Ripple Effect of Achieving Personal Goals

In the adventure of conducting private desires, the accomplishments do not exist in isolation. Quite the opposite, wearing out personal dreams has a ripple effect that extends past the person and positively impacts the own family as a whole.

Let's begin with self-self assurance, which truely grows as we make development in the path of our goals. As we artwork through our

Personal Blueprint and mark off every executed step, our self belief in our talents and capacity skyrockets. This heightened self-self guarantee is not limited to the realm of purpose success but permeates all aspects of our lives, fostering a mean experience of fulfillment and nicely-being.

But the blessings do no longer save you there. As circle of relatives members witness this non-public transformation and achievement, they too are stimulated. Seeing a sibling draw close a musical tool or a figure whole a marathon stirs motivation and strengthens the belief in the attainability of their very very own desires. In essence, the success of 1 member of the family plant life seeds of aspiration within the hearts of others, catalyzing a cycle of concept and achievement in the family.

Lastly, every non-public motive accomplished is a stride inside the path of the shared own family imaginative and prescient. Remember, the family vision is a collective of character aspirations, and each personal success brings the family one step within the course of this shared dream. This collective improvement fosters a deeper sense of concord and shared purpose within the circle of relatives, strengthening bonds and further driving person efforts.

In essence, the journey to private goal achievement isn't a solitary organisation. It's a shared voyage that uplifts the person and the family unit alike. Each personal victory contributes to a awesome cycle of suggestion, motivation, and collective development in the course of the circle of relatives imaginative and prescient. The ripple impact of personal success is therefore a powerful stress that propels the complete circle of relatives ahead, cultivating a nurturing environment of mutual increase and shared triumph.

In this financial ruin, we launched into a satisfying adventure, learning the manner to transform the summary aspirations of our vision boards into tangible, practical steps the use of a Personal Blueprint. This transformation begins with information the importance of a blueprint as a roadmap to our goals and exploring the approach of reverse engineering. We then delved into the energy inherent in the blueprint, underscoring the need for model and adjustment as we navigate existence's unpredictable currents.

Regular critiques and the birthday party of development emerged as vital components in our adventure, retaining us heading in the right direction and infusing our efforts with motivation and positivity. We additionally found the ripple impact of private success, seeing how character accomplishments enhance the whole own family's well-being and flow into us inside the route of our shared imaginative and prescient.

As we wrap up this financial ruin, we're making ready for a important pivot in our adventure: the advent of the Family Plan Blueprint. The private blueprints we have developed will form the idea for a broader, collective plan, aligning person efforts and dreams inside the large framework of our shared own family vision.

In Chapter eight, we're able to delve into the method of making a Family Plan Blueprint, taking the lessons we've found out about goal setting, contrary engineering, and blueprint creation, and using them to our collective circle of relatives imaginative and prescient. Our next circle of relatives meeting can be an exciting, palms-on session in which every member of the family's Personal Blueprint will make a contribution to a more large Family Plan. With step-via-step commands, suggestions, and examples, we're going to navigate this important way together, similarly strengthening our shared dedication to collective achievement and concord.

Chapter 8: Building The Family Plan Blueprint

In this chapter, we embark on an interesting undertaking to unite your character desires, goals, and aspirations into a unique, cohesive plan - the Family Plan Blueprint. Much like your Personal Blueprints, those plans aren't inflexible constructs but adaptable and evolving guides that accommodate the dynamism of lifestyles and the individuality of each family member. The Family Plan Blueprint captures this individuality at the same time as also highlighting the shared imaginative and prescient of your circle of relatives. This blueprint is a critical device, merging private desires with the overarching imaginative and prescient of the family, thereby fostering collective growth and success.

Gathering the Personal Blueprints

Now it is time to plot some other family meeting, the primary important step in the introduction of the Family Plan Blueprint. This process starts with amassing each family member's Personal Blueprint. These non-public courses act due to the fact the foundational building blocks to your family's overarching plan. They encompass every member's private aspirations, cautiously delineated into actionable steps, every adding their specific threads to the own family's tapestry. For this own family meeting, make sure each member comes with their Personal Blueprint, geared up to speak approximately their goals, their sub-dreams, and the every day or weekly obligations they've diagnosed.

Aligning Personal Blueprints with the Family Vision

Once you have got all of the Personal Blueprints available, the following step is aligning them with the circle of relatives's vision. This manner entails studying every Personal Blueprint and figuring out how each purpose contributes to the overall own family vision. It's a second for open dialogue and shared facts, in which each family member can see how their private aspirations weave into the circle of relatives's shared goals. This alignment creates a harmonious direction towards collective fulfillment, wherein individual achievements propel the whole family ahead.

Assembling the Family Plan Blueprint

Now comes the on the spot of synthesis. With the circle of relatives imaginative and prescient as your anchor and the Personal Blueprints as your building blocks, begin assembling the Family Plan Blueprint. Write down the own family imaginative and prescient on the pinnacle of a large piece of paper, then list each family member's important purpose under it, developing a vertical go along with the go along with the flow.

For each critical purpose, list the sub-desires and every day or weekly responsibilities associated with it, replicating the shape of the Personal Blueprints however now in a collective format. This manner lets in you to appearance how each family member's efforts make a contribution to the own family vision. This assembled Family Plan Blueprint serves as a roadmap for the circle of relatives, a visual reminder of character commitments and shared aspirations. It will manual your family's adventure closer to collective fulfillment, with every member's development feeding into the circle of relatives's normal improvement.

Like the Personal Blueprints, this Family Plan Blueprint is a dwelling report, capable of evolving as you development, face traumatic situations, and expand as a family unit. Embrace it as a photograph of your circle of relatives's concord and shared imaginative and prescient, and permit it manual you closer to a satisfying destiny.

Implementing the Family Plan Blueprint

Now that you've created your Family Plan Blueprint, the subsequent project is its implementation. Remember, the Family Plan is not great a static report, however a residing manual that ought to actively impact your every day alternatives, time table, and priorities. It is the bodily manifestation of your collective mind-set, your shared desires, and the notable behaviors you aim to domesticate as a circle of relatives.

Begin by manner of the usage of integrating the Family Plan Blueprint into your every day life. Place it in a commonplace region, somewhere without troubles visible to all own family members, so it continuously serves as a reminder of your shared vision and willpower. This visibility faucets into the power of visualization, leveraging the would probable of your unconscious mind to prioritize your family's dreams along each day obligations.

To make certain that the Family Plan Blueprint is actively guiding your family, refer lower back to it at the same time as making options. For example, if a trendy hobby or dedication arises, bear in mind whether or not or no longer or not it aligns together along with your circle of relatives's collective imaginative and prescient and the dreams listed on the Blueprint. This workout lets in keep attention and determination inside the direction of the own family imaginative and prescient and forestalls diversions from your described route.

Scheduling and prioritizing responsibilities is every different realistic manner to implement the Family Plan Blueprint. Have a weekly or bi-weekly circle of relatives meeting in that you assessment the Blueprint together. During those conferences, every member of the family can deliver updates on their Personal Blueprint progress, speak demanding conditions confronted, and have an amazing time small victories. These conferences no longer wonderful foster open conversation however additionally provide opportunities for mutual resource, feedback, and shared learning critiques.

Just like your person carrying sports are determined with the resource of your

Personal Blueprints, your circle of relatives's exercises need to reflect the shared dreams indexed on the Family Plan Blueprint. Tasks that contribute right away to the circle of relatives's vision need to be prioritized and covered into your own family's everyday everyday.

Looking lower back to Chapter 1, hold in thoughts the 3 essential elements of the Family Plan: Mindset, Behavior/Habits, and the Written Plan. The Family Plan Blueprint embodies the ones factors. Your collective mindset is captured to your shared imaginative and prescient; your shared behaviors are contemplated within the each day responsibilities and exercises you adhere to, and the written plan is your bodily Family Plan Blueprint.

Written goals are examined to significantly growth the possibilities of success. By visually displaying your Family Plan Blueprint, you are putting forward your family's self-control in your collective goals, keeping them clean in your minds and on the main fringe of your priorities.

Implementing your Family Plan Blueprint is not about achieving perfection or checking off all responsibilities right now. It's approximately creating a regular try toward your circle of relatives's imaginative and prescient, studying out of your research, and celebrating every leap forward. Remember, this adventure toward your circle of relatives's vision is a shared one, whole of mutual boom, collaboration, and a deeper records of every other. It's a adorable journey that shapes no longer truely the future of your family, however the bonds you percent these days.

The Dynamic Nature of the Family Plan Blueprint

The Family Plan Blueprint, much like your individual blueprints, is a residing, evolving file. As your circle of relatives evolves and modifications, so too have to your Family Plan Blueprint. It's critical to encompass the fluidity of this plan and recognize that adjustments and changes are not best anticipated but are a signal of growth and version.

Regularly evaluation your Family Plan Blueprint to your circle of relatives conferences. Evaluate the development made in the direction of your shared imaginative and prescient, and be open to updating or refining your dreams as events change. Perhaps an cause has been completed in advance than anticipated, or possibly a goal desires to be revised because of unexpected situations. Remember that the motive of this Blueprint is to manual and now not to limit your family's adventure.

Changes to your Family Plan Blueprint need to be a collective preference. Engage every member of the family within the dialogue and preference-making procedure to make sure every body stays aligned with and committed to the up to date plan.

Conclusion and Next Steps

Throughout this financial catastrophe, we've were given explored the importance of turning individual visions into a collective own family vision. We've seen how character dreams can align with the circle of relatives's usual purpose to create a harmonious path to shared achievement. You've moreover located out the manner to transform the ones shared aspirations right into a entire, actionable Family Plan Blueprint.

Implementing this Blueprint is in which the rubber meets the road. It's step one in turning your collective imaginative and prescient right right into a truth. However, take into account that implementation doesn't mean perfection. The purpose is development and increase, no longer faultless execution. Regularly examine and modify your Family Plan Blueprint, have an extremely good time victories big and small, and stay bendy inside the face of worrying conditions and alternate.

As we skip into the subsequent financial damage, we're capable of delve deeper into the sensible elements of reason success. We will communicate a way to prioritize duties, manipulate your time table, and music your improvement. We might also additionally equip you with strategies to address setbacks and keep your motivation excessive at some stage in this adventure.

Get organized to take the subsequent essential stride towards your own family's imaginative and prescient. In Chapter nine, we can find out the way to translate the desires specified in your Family Plan Blueprint into actionable steps. You'll examine strategies for effective project prioritization, realistic scheduling, and constant improvement tracking. In this financial ruin, we are able to additionally address the disturbing situations that unavoidably rise up in this route, providing you with sensible techniques to adjust your plans as needed, cope with setbacks, and keep momentum in the direction of your collective family imaginative and prescient. The adventure maintains, so allow's flip those desires into motion.

Chapter 9: Turning Goals Into Action

At this juncture, you have got installation your Family Plan Blueprint and person Personal Blueprints. You have your imaginative and prescient smooth and your desires set. Now, it's time to delve deeper into the mechanics of success. In this segment, we're in a position to speak the vital idea of actionable steps.

Actionable steps are the smaller, concrete duties which you undertake to attain your large dreams. Think of them because the bricks that assemble the course toward your goals. They spoil down an intimidating, massive purpose into viable, practical obligations. These steps are the essence of ways we turn our imaginative and prescient into fact.

Translating the dreams out of your Family Plan Blueprint or Personal Blueprint into actionable steps includes a piece of opposite engineering.

You begin with the endpoint in mind – your purpose – and then you parent out the right obligations required to get you there.

At times, you could discover yourself at a loss on how to break down a sub-motive. Don't fear, that is part of the technique. When you run into such gaps or question marks on your Blueprint, take it as a signal to do greater studies. Search the net, look at books, talk to specialists, or are seeking advice from mentors. Remember, every question mark you cope with strengthens your Blueprint, paving a clearer direction closer to your intention.

In this adventure of contrary engineering your desires into actionable steps, you'll possibly comprehend that it is not a linear system. Sometimes, you can need to revisit your steps, refine them, or maybe add new ones as you discover greater facts or benefit new insights.

Remember, your Blueprint isn't set in stone; it's miles a dwelling, evolving manual. Being open to adjustments is a key a part of fulfillment. So, dive in, begin breaking down your desires, and mild up the route on your goals with actionable steps.

Prioritizing Tasks

After transforming your goals into actionable steps, you're left with a huge number of obligations. Each of these duties is a chunk of the puzzle, an critical step in the path of reaching your desires. However, they're not all same in urgency or significance. This is wherein prioritization comes into play.

Effective prioritization is an crucial tool to your purpose success toolkit. It allows you interest your power on duties which can be maximum pressing, most important, and maximum impactful in the direction of your goals. It prevents you from being beaten with the useful resource of your project list and allows make certain you are making tremendous improvement. Here's how you could prioritize your obligations:

Importance vs. Urgency:

The first step in prioritizing obligations is distinguishing between importance and urgency. Urgent obligations name for instant hobby. They're regularly associated with drawing near deadlines, and no longer addressing them may additionally have right away consequences. Important responsibilities, but, won't require on the spot attention however are sizeable for prolonged-term intention achievement.

The Eisenhower Matrix is a beneficial device for this undertaking differentiation. It divides tasks into four instructions:

Urgent and Important

Important however Not Urgent

Urgent however Not Important

Not Urgent and Not Important

This categorization will allow you to understand what duties you want to attention on now, time desk for later, delegate, or perhaps take away.

Contribution to Goals:

A challenge's importance frequently lies in how thousands it contributes to achieving your overarching desires. Reflect on each assignment and ask, "How a good deal does finishing this undertaking pass me or us inside the path of our purpose?"

Tasks which have a exceptional effect on goal success need to simply accept better priority.

Effort vs. Impact:

Another thing to keep in thoughts whilst prioritizing duties is the attempt-to-effect ratio. Some responsibilities require a whole lot of strive but yield little development in the course of your reason. Others might take a bargain much less time and strength but have a top notch impact in your cause fulfillment. Aim to prioritize excessive-impact, low-try obligations to make green development.

Deadlines:

Some obligations include integrated deadlines, specifically the ones associated with out of doors elements which encompass college assignments or artwork projects. Be privy to those time limits and make sure that you plan your task time desk consequently.

Remember, the objective of prioritizing duties isn't to create a rigid shape but to provide a manual to help you attention your efforts effectively. Priorities can exchange as your events, facts, or goals trade. Be bendy and inclined to re-have a look at your priorities frequently to make certain they align together with your cutting-edge truth and desires.

Now, ready with the ones prioritization strategies, check your actionable obligations. Organize and rank them in keeping with their importance, urgency, and contribution for your goals. This will offer you with a easy route of movement closer to cause fulfillment.

Creating a Schedule

With prioritized duties handy, the subsequent step is to create a practical time desk. A properly-perception-out agenda serves as your roadmap for motion, making sure all and sundry is jogging on their duties systematically and purposefully. Here are a few pointers to create an effective time table:

Start with Fixed Commitments: Begin via mapping out the consistent commitments like university hours, work schedules, food, sleep, and ordinary family meetings. These time slots are usually non-negotiable and provide a form to plan spherical.

Assign Time for Prioritized Tasks: Next, allocate precise time slots on your prioritized duties. Be practical about how masses you could reap in a day and avoid the temptation to over-time table. Remember, it's far more useful to finish one undertaking very well than to in element do numerous.

Balance Work and Relaxation: A balanced time table consists of time for rest and enjoyment. This is as essential as time for duties because it prevents burnout and lets in keep prolonged-time period motivation. Make positive each member of the family has time for pursuits, rest, and socializing.

Use Tools: Tools like day planners or digital calendars can be very beneficial. They assist you to visualize your time desk, set reminders, and make changes with out problem.

Stay Flexible: Understand that your time desk is a guide, now not a inflexible form. Life is unpredictable, and you can need to regulate your time table for sudden sports or responsibilities that take longer than expected.

Create a Routine: Lastly, motive to create a ordinary. Routines streamline sports activities sports, reduce selection fatigue, and increase overall performance.

Tracking Progress

To journey towards your goals, it's critical to understand in that you stand, what you have got got finished, and what lies in advance. This is wherein improvement tracking comes into play. Here are a few effective strategies:

Use a Progress Chart or Journal: Visual gear like a improvement chart or mag can be exceptionally motivating. They provide a clean photo of what you've got finished, and seeing your obligations getting ticked off can give you a sense of pride and momentum.

Digital Tools: You can also use digital equipment for improvement tracking. Numerous apps allow you to music responsibilities, set reminders, or even percentage your improvement with others.

Regular Check-ins: Regular own family conferences need to encompass development check-ins. These offer an possibility for each family member to share their accomplishments, struggles, and plans. They foster a sense of shared development, mutual beneficial aid, and collective party.

Celebrate Victories: No matter variety amount how small, have fun each accomplishment. This reinforces a incredible association with project very last touch and boosts motivation. Celebrations can be as easy as acknowledging the strive in a circle of relatives meeting or planning a small treat.

Remember, the cause of tracking improvement isn't to create pressure however to manual growth, facilitate hassle-solving, and create a pleasing environment of obligation and birthday celebration. It's a optimistic way of studying, adjusting, and enhancing.

With a realistic schedule and improvement tracking machine in area, you're nicely-ready to reveal your desires into actions and pass in the direction of your anticipated future, each as people and as a circle of relatives unit. Let's preserve this journey inside the subsequent financial disaster, wherein we're going to discover techniques to preserve motivation and manage setbacks.

Chapter 10: Nurturing Persistence And Resilience

Every worthwhile journey is marked with the aid of obstacles and setbacks, and the direction to undertaking your non-public and own family goals isn't any exception. If we take a look at the narratives of the maximum a hit human beings and households, they're frequently whole of memories of staying power inside the face of adversity. They did now not make it to their dreams because of the reality they have been lucky or because of the fact they had it clean. Instead, they had been given there because of the fact they were resilient, and they endured even if faced with barriers.

Persistence is the unwavering determination to maintain toward your motive, irrespective of the hurdles that come your manner. It is prepared staying committed to the journey, even if it is hard. Resilience, on the other hand, is the ability to get better from setbacks, to investigate from failures, and to conform to changes. It is ready getting higher speedy from issues and the use of them as stepping stones in vicinity of obstacles.

As we work through our Family Plan Blueprint and Individual Blueprints, we want to apprehend and take transport of that there is probably disturbing conditions. Some obligations may additionally take longer than predicted, surprising limitations would possibly probable arise, and there also can additionally be moments whilst our motivation wanes. These are all ordinary additives of the way, now not signs and symptoms of failure. They are valuable possibilities for getting to know and boom.

When confronted with setbacks, a resilient circle of relatives would not see it as a vain-stop but as a detour. They have a examine what prompted the setback, research from it, adjust their plan as essential, and keep transferring ahead. Persistence continues the family pushing beforehand, at the same time as resilience allows them to get better and turn out to be more potent whenever they face adversity.

By cultivating persistence and resilience in the own family, we are not best increasing our possibilities of undertaking our collective vision however additionally building competencies at the manner to serve us properly in all regions of life. In the following sections, we're able to delve into the techniques we are capable of nurture those vital attributes and make certain that we live inspired and capable of overcoming any traumatic conditions that come our way.

Fostering a Growth Mindset

The concept of a boom thoughts-set turned into developed via psychologist Carol Dweck and is precious to fostering staying electricity and resilience. In essence, a growth mind-set is the perception that talents and intelligence can be advanced via determination, tough art work, and a love of gaining knowledge of. It's a belief within the electricity of "however" — you could now not be capable of do a little thing now, however that does not suggest you can now not be capable of do it inside the future.

When we foster a boom attitude inner our families, we start to view worrying situations not as threats but as opportunities to growth and analyze. We begin to see attempt as a direction to mastery instead of a chore. We discover ways to embody remarks, even if it is first rate complaint, because of the truth we recognize that it allows us decorate. We grow to be extra resilient because of the reality we understand that setbacks are an important a part of the gaining knowledge of approach, not evidence of our lack of capacity.

Cultivating a growth mind-set involves shifting the way we suppose and talk about talents and achievements. Instead of pronouncing "I'm not accurate at this," we can say "I'm no longer extraordinary at this, however." Instead of praising outcomes, we praise attempt, technique, and development. Instead of shying faraway from worrying conditions, we encompass them as possibilities for boom.

Here are some techniques to foster a increase attitude inside your family:

Make reading a circle of relatives price. Encourage interest and the pursuit of latest capabilities and information, whether or now not it aligns straight away in conjunction with your desires or no longer. Foster a love for mastering for its personal sake.

Embrace stressful conditions: When faced with a tough challenge, body it as an opportunity to look at and increase in preference to an impediment. Encourage every distinct to take on traumatic conditions and to persist in the face of setbacks.

Use boom-oriented language: The terms we use can shape our mind-set. Use language that fosters boom, like "but," "studies," "growth," and "enhance." Instead of announcing, "I failed," say, "I observed out."

Celebrate try and improvement: Instead of in truth celebrating while a purpose is reached, have fun the attempt placed into reaching it and the progress made alongside the way. This reinforces the idea that effort and getting to know are precious in and of themselves, now not honestly as approach to an end.

Model a growth thoughts-set: As dad and mom or older family people, you may lead by way of instance. Show your personal dedication to getting to know and growth, percent your personal traumatic situations and the way you overcame them, and exhibit that it's adequate not to comprehend the whole thing and to make mistakes.

By fostering a increase attitude inner your circle of relatives, you will be nurturing an environment in which staying power, resilience, and continuous reading are the norm. This attitude is probably a effective device as you figure together to expose your circle of relatives and personal blueprints into truth.

Strategies for Staying Motivated

Maintaining motivation over the long time, especially while pursuing large goals, may be a undertaking. However, there are several strategies that you may rent as a circle of relatives to stay stimulated and keep momentum. Here are a few key ones to keep in mind:

Use Positive Affirmations: Positive affirmations are statements that you repeat to yourself, designed to have an impact in your conscious and unconscious thoughts. They can help to encourage you, preserve your awareness for your dreams, and conquer horrible mind. Examples may embody: "I can try this," "Every step brings me towards my aim," or "I am capable of accomplishing my dreams." You can also use affirmations which may be precise in your goals.

Create Visual Reminders: Our surroundings have to have a big have an effect on on our mind-set and motivation. Placing visual reminders of your goals and development in visible places can be a powerful motivational device. These can take the form of your Personal and Family Blueprints, development charts, photos symbolizing your dreams, or inspirational quotes. Seeing the ones reminders each day can help to maintain your desires at the forefront of your thoughts and inspire you to do so.

Lean on Family Support: As a family working closer to a shared vision, you have got got got a completely unique supply of assist and motivation — each different. Make a dependancy of sharing your successes and disturbing situations for your circle of relatives meetings, and offer every other encouragement and reward. Knowing that you're all in this together can be a powerful motivator.

Remember, motivation isn't a one-time occasion, however a device that you need to nurture constantly. It's perfectly normal to have usaand downs. The secret is to maintain going, hold a extremely good mindset, and make use of those strategies to help gas your motivation on the adventure closer to your dreams.

Overcoming Challenges Together

The journey towards accomplishing your desires, both in my opinion and as a own family, will not be with out its traumatic conditions. Obstacles, setbacks, and hurdles are an inevitable part of the gadget. However, those stressful situations do not have to derail your improvement. In truth, they may be effective catalysts for growth, studying, and strengthening your family bonds. Here's how you could cope with challenges collectively as a own family:

Approach Challenges as Opportunities: Start thru fostering a collective thoughts-set that views demanding conditions no longer as insurmountable roadblocks however as possibilities for boom and learning. Each undertaking you encounter can train you some thing valuable, whether or not or now not it's far a cutting-edge technique, a personal energy you failed to recognize you had, or a better expertise of what does no longer work. Embrace those opportunities to research and develop.

Practice Problem-Solving Strategies: As worrying situations upward thrust up, use them as an possibility to exercise and decorate your family's hassle-solving capabilities. This would possibly probably include brainstorming feasible solutions, assessing the specialists and cons of various strategies, trying out out an answer, after which reflecting on the consequences. Remember, it is not approximately getting it great the primary time, however approximately mastering and improving over the years.

Emphasize Open Communication: Open and honest communique is pinnacle to efficiently coping with and overcoming demanding situations. Encourage each member of the family to specific their mind, feelings, and issues with out worry of judgment. When each person feels heard and valued, you are more likely to give you effective answers that everyone is devoted to.

Support Each Other: Challenges can from time to time feel overwhelming, however don't forget which you're now not in this alone. As a circle of relatives, you are a group, and there is a unique electricity in that. Be there for each different at a few degree in the hard instances. Offer phrases of encouragement, lend a listening ear, or without a doubt offer a comforting hug. Your guide can supply each unique the electricity to maintain going.

Overcoming challenges together not first-rate permits you bypass beforehand toward your desires, however it moreover strengthens your own family unit. It fosters resilience, deepens your information of each other, and cultivates a enjoy of shared accomplishment that might in addition fuel your motivation. Remember, it's miles not the absence of annoying situations that defines your achievement, however the way you reply to them.

Practicing Patience

One of the most essential components of conducting your dreams is persistence. The gadget of figuring out goals and making sizable modifications does not get up in a single day; it calls for everyday attempt over a period of time. There's a well-known saying that 'Rome wasn't built in an afternoon,' and the same precept applies on your family's dreams.

Consider your goals and the associated obligations as a marathon, now not a dash. The concept is to hold a normal pace that permits for consistency and avoids burnout. It's crucial to keep in mind that small, ordinary steps within the course of your goals can gather into great development over the years.

Encourage every family member to understand that setbacks or slower development than anticipated aren't indicators of failure, however as an opportunity an crucial part of the journey inside the path of fulfillment. Let every setback serve as a lesson and each delay a reminder of the importance of staying strength and the candy taste of difficult-earned fulfillment.

This bankruptcy supplied insights into the essential function that staying power, resilience, and staying power play in the journey in the direction of reaching your goals. We discussed the significance of fostering a growth attitude, strategies to stay inspired, and techniques to conquer annoying conditions collectively as a family.

Remember that disturbing situations and setbacks are not barriers, but stepping stones on the path to growth and achievement. As a circle of relatives, your collective electricity, help, and determination will assist you navigate any barriers that come your way.

As we improvement thru this journey, typically hold in thoughts the imaginative and prescient you've got created for your family. Your shared dreams, your collective vision, and your perseverance are effective equipment that, while combined, can bring about excellent alternate and growth.

Stay robust, live resilient, and most significantly, don't forget to have an amazing time each small victory alongside the manner. The adventure within the route of your desires is simply as essential due to the fact the vacation spot.

Chapter 11: The Ongoing Process

As we journey toward the conclusion of this manual, it's far essential to don't forget that the arrival and implementation of the Family Plan isn't a one-time event. Instead, it's far an ongoing device, just like a street experience. Just as a street adventure calls for regular tests on the map, fuel levels, and car situations, the adventure within the route of attaining your circle of relatives desires wishes constant evaluations and updates.

Your Family Plan isn't carved in stone. It is a dwelling, respiratory file that evolves with you, adapting to the changing tides of your circle of relatives's needs, aspirations, and occasions. It's a device that serves you, no longer the possibility way spherical. Therefore, it need to be bendy enough to residence shifts in your own family's dynamics or new desires that might rise up.

You ought to aim to have ordinary evaluations of the Family Plan, preferably in the course of your weekly or biweekly own family conferences. During those evaluations, communicate the progress made, any demanding situations encountered, and the following steps for every aim. If crucial, make adjustments for your plan to better serve your dreams or accommodate any unexpected conditions. Remember, the intention isn't to paste rigidly to the plan, but to use it as a compass that guides your family within the path of its shared imaginative and prescient.

Celebrating Progress

In the midst of the hustle and bustle of chasing our goals, it's far clean to lose sight of the manner an extended manner we have come. Celebration is a essential a part of the journey that often receives overlooked. Recognizing and celebrating development, irrespective of how small, plays a essential position in preserving motivation and fostering a incredible circle of relatives surroundings.

When each member of the family shares their improvement inside the own family conferences, make it a point to have amusing their achievements. This can be as smooth as a spherical of applause, a unique dinner, or maybe a small token of popularity. It might now not rely how large or small the gesture is. What subjects is the message it sends: "We see your strive, we fee your contributions, and we're pleased with you."

Recognizing progress reinforces a excessive incredible comments loop of achievement and reward. It serves to inspire and inspire every family member to keep pushing ahead. Furthermore, it creates an surroundings of encouragement and positivity, that's beneficial to all people's mental nicely-being. Celebrations remind us that the journey toward reaching our goals may be amusing, profitable, and whole of moments of pleasure and satisfaction.

Impact on Family Life

As we take a 2nd to step decrease lower back and reflect, it is important to remember the profound, prolonged-term impact this exercise may additionally should your circle of relatives lifestyles. Implementing the Family Plan and maintaining the place to have a have a look at via isn't always just about task person or collective desires. It's about the approach and the lasting, transformative results this adventure may have for your circle of relatives.

First and critical, the Family Plan can appreciably supply a boost to own family bonds. By working collectively in the course of not unusual targets, you're fostering a subculture of teamwork and shared cause. The circle of relatives conferences turn out to be a shared ritual, a time to return collectively, to connect and engage with every one-of-a-type. They provide a platform for every family member to voice their hopes, desires, fears, and frustrations in a secure, supportive environment. This collective revel in can significantly beautify the texture of concord and cohesion amongst own family people.

Secondly, this machine can immensely decorate conversation inside the circle of relatives. By often discussing goals, improvement, and stressful conditions, you are encouraging open and honest communicate. This workout can assist destroy down boundaries, enhance understanding, and foster empathy. It gives an possibility for every family member to specific themselves, to be heard, and to be understood. Over time, this could lead to better war decision, deeper mutual apprehend, and stronger relationships.

Finally, the Family Plan allows personal and collective growth. By putting dreams and mapping out the stairs to gain them, every member of the family is actively running towards self-development and private fulfillment. Simultaneously, the circle of relatives as a whole is developing, getting to know, and evolving collectively. You're collectively growing a destiny that aligns along with your shared vision, reinforcing the fact that you're all in this collectively.

In essence, the Family Plan Blueprint is greater than satisfactory a roadmap to carrying out desires. It's a tool for building a stronger, extra related own family unit. It encourages open conversation, fosters mutual recognize, and promotes private and collective boom. The splendor of this journey is that it adapts as your circle of relatives evolves, usually serving as a manual within the course of your shared imaginative and prescient and aspirations.

As you keep in this journey, may also your direction be packed with shared victories, joyous celebrations, and moments of growth and studying. Remember, the actual value lies now not definitely within the vacation spot, but in the adventure you embark on collectively as a own family.

Final Thoughts and Encouragement

In the begin, we in assessment navigating thru the chaos of existence without a solid Family Plan to a battlefield in which infantrymen wandered aimlessly, each remoted and uncertain of the venture to be had. It's a colourful, possibly excessive, metaphor, but it's far apt in highlighting the disarray that could occur even as a family tries to navigate existence's demanding situations with out smooth dreams, powerful conversation, and a shared vision.

Throughout this ebook, we've got got have been given methodically crafted the Family Plan, jogging collectively to foster a shared mindset, expand wonderful behaviors and conduct, and to location all of it collectively in a concrete, written plan—a blueprint for achievement. This file has been transformed from a clean canvas to a residing, respiration testament for your family's shared vision, hopes, and goals.

Now, you stand collectively as a family, no longer wandering aimlessly on an unforgiving battlefield, but marching purposefully, issue by way of using facet, towards shared desires and fulfillment. You've superior a warfare plan, a unified approach, to be able to guide you through the complex terrain of life. It's now not approximately each soldier—or family member—attempting to live on on their private, however about moving together as a unit, leveraging the strength of the collective to gain greater than the sum of its factors.

It's important to undergo in mind that this journey may not give up proper right here. Just as squaddies continuously train, analyze, and adapt to converting activities, your Family Plan Blueprint will evolve with you. It's a dynamic, bendy tool designed that will help you navigate life's ever-converting panorama. It should be reviewed, adjusted, and delicate as times change, as dreams evolve, and as you are making improvement.

Chapter 12: What Are Family Planning Methods?

Family planning can be defined as the practice of controlling the number of children born from a couple or person, as well as the time frame between pregnancies. It involves the use of contraception, as well as the promotion of family life education, pre-conception counseling, management of STDs, etc.

Family planning allows people to attain their desired number of children and determine the spacing of pregnancies. It is achieved through use of contraceptive methods and the treatment of infertility.

To sum up, the following are the three main goals of family planning methods:

To let people choose when is the right moment for them to have offspring

To allow people to decide upon the number of children they wish to have

To let people decide on the time frame between pregnancies, that is, the age gap between siblings

These purposes can be achieved thanks to contraceptive or birth control methods and infertility treatments.

Other aspects addressed by family planning are:

Sexuality education

Prevention and treatment of sexually transmitted diseases (STDs)

Counseling for pregnancy and birth

Assisted Reproductive Technology (ART)

Why are they so important?

Family planning is a fundamental right, and as such, if done properly, it offers multiple advantages for women and their families, as well as for our society in general.

In developing countries, reproductive life planning can even save lives, and contribute to the overall wellbeing of the society.

In short, it brings a series of benefits for everyone and contributes to family happiness. The following are the most significant ones:

Reduced infant mortality rates

Especially among less-than-1-year-old babies due to maternal health problems or after having babies too close together. A 2-year gap between pregnancies helps women deliver healthier children, and increases the infant mortality rate by 50%.

Prevention of unplanned or high-risk pregnancies

Limiting the number of pregnancies a woman goes through, as well as the time frame between them, the overall maternal health and wellbeing increase. Likewise, when the number of babies a woman carries is limited to her childbearing years, the maternal mortality rate (MMRate) decreases.

Prevention of HIV transmission

Firstly, it helps to prevent the risk of unplanned pregnancy in HIV-infected women, which at the same time helps prevent the mother-to-child transmission of HIV, reducing the orphan statistics. Secondly, barrier birth control methods like the condom offer added protection, as they prevent unwanted pregnancies and the transmission of STDs like the HIV all at the same time.

Reduced incidence of abortion complications

Since family planning contributes to reducing the rate of unintended pregnancies, it is only logical that it also diminishes the abortion rate, which currently represents 13% of the world's MMRate.

Diminished rate of adolescent pregnancies

Babies born from too young girls have a higher chance of being born prematurely or with low birth weight. Moreover, children born from teenagers have a higher neonatal mortality rate (NMR). It reduces the school drop-out rate as well.

Decreased population growth

Family planning helps to control the world's birth rates and reduce overpopulation, which contributes to improving important areas such as the economy, environment, and sustainable development.

Power to decide and better sex education

A person who is well-educated can make better decisions when it comes to dealing with her overall health and wellbeing.

Spreading as many information as necessary to prevent the absence of proper family planning is crucial to achieve the well-being of both partners, facilitate personal autonomy, support reproductive health, and improve the development and growth of our society.

Family planning tips

When a couple or woman decides to get pregnant, the next step is to start taking the necessary steps towards achieving a healthy pregnancy above all.

First and foremost, in order to increase the chances of getting pregnant, one should learn how to calculate her fertile days and engage into unprotected sexual intercourse during those days.

Secondly, we recommend that you pay special attention to the following tips, all of them related to maternal health during pregnancy and the overall wellbeing of the pregnant woman when she is trying to conceive (TTC):

Start taking folic acid. This vitamin helps prevent congenital spine and spinal cord malformations, including spina bifida. The intake of folic acid is especially important throughout the first trimester of pregnancy.

Follow a balanced diet, high in fiber, iron, calcium, omega-3 fats, etc.

Leave behind any toxic habit you may have, including tobacco and alcohol consumption. Caffeine is also unadvisable.

Make an appointment with your OB/GYN for a gynecological exam and to receive the first recommendations for a healthy pregnancy.

Do moderate physical activity. Sports like yoga, pilates, swimming, or walking are strongly recommended.

Full compliance with mandatory vaccination schedules is crucial to being immunized. Get yourself vaccinated if you missed one or more doses when you were younger.

Take special care of your intimate hygiene, and practice good hygiene in general now more than ever.

If you have not had toxoplasmosis ever before, do not eat unwashed fruits or vegetables. Also, avoid eating raw or insufficiently cooked meat unless they have been previously frozen at a -22 °C temperature for 10 days.

Avoid, as long as possible, exposure to chemical agents and environmental contaminants in general. Working at a gas station or dry-cleaning shops may be perjudicial.

Do not start medications without medical prescription and consent, including over-the-counter drugs.

If followed by both the man and the woman without becoming obsessed, these tips are the first steps towards bringing a healthy baby into the world.

Types of family planning methods

Assisted Reproductive Technology (ART)

Fertility treatments are used to help someone become a parent when it is not possible naturally, and as such they are considered family planning methods as well.

As in the case of contraception, we can find a varied range of fertility options, each one of them indicated depending on the cause of infertility. The following are the most popular ones:

Artificial Insemination (AI)

It consists in inserting the processed semen sample provided by the partner or husband directly inside the woman's womb. Ovarian stimulation is required to monitor the moment of ovulation.

In Vitro Fertilization (IVF)

The eggs of the patient are harvested by means of follicle puncture (ovum pick-up) after inducing ovulation. After that, they are fertilized with the husband's or partner's sperm in the lab. The resulting embryos will be cultured prior to transferring those with the best quality to the womb so that they are hopefully able to attach.

Egg donation

In this case, the method of choice is IVF as well, but this time it is not the patient's eggs which are used, but those from an egg donor. Certain diseases, poor egg quality, or low ovarian reserve are the most common causes why a woman may need to use donor eggs to get pregnant.

Preimplantation Genetic Diagnosis (PGD)

This type of embryo genetic testing is used to examine the embryos obtained after IVF. The goal is to discard those containing chromosomal alterations and transfer only the healthy ones. It is used to prevent the transmission of genetic abnormalities to offspring as well.

Finally, fertility preservation is another family planning option that should be considered in those cases where it might be necessary. When a woman or man of childbearing age decides to postpone parenthood, freezing their gametes is a highly recommended option, since the biological clock is ticking, especially in the case of women.

What tips should a woman follow who wants to get pregnant?

Pregnancy planning is one of the most important moments for a couple, and in many occasions it implies a certain stress for the future parents, who usually have many doubts at this time.

Nowadays, it is recommended to plan the pregnancy, because apart from making it come at the best psycho-social time for the couple (which helps responsible parenthood), some measures can be carried out within the medical field itself that will help the pregnancy to pass normally, avoiding unnecessary risks. These measures are:

Health examination

Start of folic acid intake

Decreasing stress

Assessing the woman's age

What is family planning operation?

Family planning operation for women is called tubal ligation or tubectomy. It means that the Fallopian tubes are ligated, thereby blocking the passage of sperm. In other words, sperm cannot reach the egg, and fertilization won't occur. It is a permanent birth control method, and for this reason it should be done only if one is sure not to have children in the future.

Can family planning pills terminate pregnancy?

No, birth control pills (oral contraception) cannot be used to terminate a pregnancy. They work by stopping the ovaries from releasing an egg and also thicken the cervical mucus, thereby making it difficult for the sperm to live and swim inside the female reproductive tract.

Get information about this hormonal birth control method and other contraceptive options here: Types of Birth Control Methods.

Does family planning bring down fertility?

There exists a long-running debate on this issue. Actually, with a few exceptions, women are able to get their fertility (ovulation cycle) back immediately after they stop using birth control. The level of fertility depends on your age above all, as well as on other things that actually have nothing to do with the use of contraception.

Does family planning stop menstruation?

No, a woman continues to have her periods in spite of the use of contraception. However, they can be used to delay your period or choose when you want it to start each month.

To put it simply, birth control pills work by "imitating" the natural menstrual cycle, and this is the reason why women who use them still experience bleeding similar to that of periods, although it is not an actual period.

A pack of birth control pills contains 28 pills, out of which only 21 are active pills (i.e. they contain hormones). Inactive pills are actually a placebo used to maintain the routine of taking one pill each day.

The woman will experience bleeding during the days when she is taking the inactive pills. This bleeding occurs as a response of the body to stopping the reception of the hormones that where present on the active pills.

Is family planning allowed in Islam?

Yes, as long as it is used as a private measure to regulate the family size due to economic or health reasons.

As for consent to use it between husband and wife, according to Islamic law, the woman has full right to use birth control methods, even without the consent of her husband.

However, she cannot force her spouse to use a condom or practice the pull-out method if he does not want to.

Does family planning cause weight gain?

Actually, there is no reason why, in spite of the common belief. But it is true that, though rarely, some women do gain a little weight after starting taking oral contraceptives. It is due to fluid retention, which means that it is just a temporary side effect.

Why is family planning important?

Knowing whether you do or don't want to have children in the next few years can help you and your partner prepare for conception or choose appropriate contraception.

If you're already parents, family planning takes on new meaning. Having another child will change your family's lives. Are you and your partner ready to take care of a newborn again? How will your other child or children react to sharing your attention with a new baby?

The timing of your pregnancies is important, too. While you and your partner might have preferences about how close in age you'd like your children to be, some research shows that how you space your pregnancies can affect mother and baby.

What are the risks of spacing pregnancies too close together?

Research suggests that beginning a pregnancy within six months of a live birth is associated with an increased risk of:

Premature birth

The placenta partially or completely peeling away from the inner wall of the uterus before delivery (placental abruption)

Low birth weight

Congenital disorders

Schizophrenia

Maternal anemia

In addition, recent research suggests that closely spaced pregnancies might be associated with an increased risk of autism in second-born children. The risk is highest for pregnancies spaced less than 12 months apart.

Closely spaced pregnancies might not give a mother enough time to recover from pregnancy before moving on to the next. For example, pregnancy and breastfeeding can deplete your stores of nutrients, particularly folate. If you become pregnant before replacing those stores, it could affect your health or your baby's health. Inflammation of the genital tract that develops during pregnancy and doesn't completely heal before the next pregnancy could also play a role.

Are there risks associated with spacing pregnancies too far apart?

Some research also suggests that long intervals between pregnancies pose concerns for mothers and babies, such as an increased risk of preeclampsia in people with no history of the condition.

It's not clear why long pregnancy intervals might cause health problems. It's possible that pregnancy improves uterine capacity to promote fetal growth and support, but that over time these beneficial physiological changes disappear.

What's the best interval between pregnancies?

To reduce the risk of pregnancy complications and other health problems, research suggests waiting 18 to 24 months but less than five years after a live birth before attempting your next pregnancy. Balancing concerns about infertility, people older than 35 might consider waiting 12 months before becoming pregnant again.

The risks and recommendations don't apply to couples who have had a miscarriage. If you're healthy and feel ready, there's no need to wait to conceive after a miscarriage.

Choosing when to have another baby is a personal decision. When planning your next pregnancy, you and your partner might consider various factors in addition to the health risks and benefits. Until you make a decision about when to have another child, use a reliable method of birth control.

What else do I need to know about pregnancy spacing?

There's no perfect time to have another baby. Even with careful planning, you can't always control when conception happens. However, discussing reliable birth control options until you are ready to conceive and understanding the possible risks associated with the timing of your pregnancies can help you make an informed decision about when to grow your family.

9 TYPES OF FAMILY PLANNING | BIRTH CONTROL METHODS

Unprotected sex significantly increases the chances of pregnancy. Sex is a hormonal requirement of the human body, but pregnancy is not. Pregnancy is a beautiful phase, but only when one is ready. Unwanted pregnancy is related to a 20 – 22% increase in mental health issues. Not only does it affects mentally, but can also lead to health issues. This is why it is important to educate yourself about the different types of family planning.

Also, known as contraception or birth control methods, the types of family planning range from natural methods to surgical methods. Contraception methods are necessary for both males and females, to avoid pregnancy and other sex-related diseases, such as HIV/AIDs.

Adhering to the importance of education on contraception methods, here in this blog we will take you through nine types of family planning. These methods are effective and safe.

Barrier Methods

Barrier methods are not permanent types of family planning. They include cervical caps, condoms for both men and women and vaginal sponges.

Cervical Caps

Contraceptive caps are made of silicone and fit snugly at the cervix, that's why the name – cervical caps. These caps prevent the fertilisation of eggs and sperm. Cervical caps prevent the sperm from entering the uterus and thereby giving protection against unwanted pregnancy. Use the cervical caps along with spermicides (comes in the form of gel, foam, cream and pessaries., used to kill sperms.)

Condoms

Condoms come for both males and females. Male condoms are to be rolled over the penis, while the female condom goes inside the vagina (open end outwards, and closed one inside). Condoms are one of the best types of family planning. Usually made of latex or polyurethane, condoms form a barrier between sperm and eggs. According to WHO reports, the effectiveness of condoms is — 2 out of 100 females with consistent use of male condoms, and 5 out of 100 women with female condoms. Plus, it is the only method that acts as protection against sex-borne diseases and unwanted pregnancies.

Natural Methods

On average, women go through 6 fertility days including ovulation day. This duration is ideal for those willing to have a child, while for others, there are natural types of family planning methods that pinpoint the time of fertility. This information can be later used to avoid pregnancy.

Rhythm Method

Believed to be one of the oldest types of family planning methods, it is based on the menstruation calendar. Usually, the menstruation cycle goes on for 28-30 days, and ovulation happens on the 14th day since the cycle starts. Thus you have the highest fertility on the 12th, 13th, and 14th day. So, to use this method, one should avoid having unprotected sex between 8 to 19 days of the mensuration cycle. You can make a chart for your cycle and keep track of the same. This method is only effective for women with regular period cycles.

Ovulation Method

The ovulation method, also known as the cervical mucus method, is one of the predictive types of family planning. In the method, you have to track the mucus made by the cervix. When you are ovulating, the mucus is wet, clear, stretchy, and appears to be like raw egg white. Make a chart of the mucus discretion to avoid having sex around fertility and ovulation days.

Surgical methods

These are considered the permanent types of family planning. There are only 0.1 women per 100 with a chance to get pregnant after vasectomy or female sterilisation.

Vasectomy

Vasectomy is a surgical contraceptive method for males. The surgery usually takes about 15 – 20 minutes and is performed under local anaesthesia. Also known as male sterilisation, in this method, the tubes carrying sperm to the male testicles are cut, blocked or sealed. With a 99% effective rate, vasectomy prevents sperm from entering the seminal fluid, making it one of the best types of family planning. The surgery itself is painless and quick, and once done, who won't have to worry about contraception, ever again!

Female Sterilisation

Similar to male sterilisation or vasectomy, female sterilisation blocks the fallopian tubes. These tubes connect the ovaries to the uterus and when blocked, they prevent the sperm from reaching the egg. Depending upon the method used for sterilisation, you just have to use protection or contraception till a week after surgery or till your next period. Female sterilisation has a 99% effectiveness rate, plus, it doesn't cause any nuance in your sex life or period cycle.

IUD

IUD, intrauterine device – is a device made of copper or plastic with a low dosage of progestin. For this method, you first have to go through a cervix examination, once the reports are approved by your doctor, you can opt for IUD or better referred to as one of the best types of family planning. It is placed inside your uterus by a trained professional. Once it is inserted, you won't have to worry about contraception. IUD can be used for three to ten years.

Hormonal Methods

Hormonal methods use your hormones to avoid pregnancy. These types of family planning methods need a prescription from your doctor, and will either contain only one or both progestin and estrogen.

Birth Control Pills

These pills are to be taken only after a professional prescribes them. Birth control pills can either have both estrogen and progestin, or only progestin. They prevent ovulation and are one of the safest and best types of family planning. You have to take the same pill at the same time, every day. While they are pretty effective when taken exactly as prescribed, birth control pills can cause breast tenderness and nausea, at times.

Vaginal Rings

It is understandable from its name that this method is for females. Vaginal rings are to be used for a period of 21 days, then with a week's break, you have to insert them again. These rings are small and made of soft plastic. Once it is placed in your vagina, it will release oestrogen and progestogen and make it difficult for the sperm to reach the egg, thereby preventing pregnancy.

We hope that this blog helps you learn about the different types of family planning and their effectiveness. All of the above-mentioned methods are proven effective by professionals, Make sure to keep your gynaecologist in the loop while taking these measures to avoid any side effects.

Chapter 13: Permanent Family Planning Methods

Sterilisation is the most effective, and one of the most widely used contraceptive methods available worldwide. It is often the best contraceptive choice when desired family size has been achieved. Both tubal ligation in women, and vasectomy in men, are one-time procedures that are safe, inexpensive and relatively straightforward to do for a trained person. Sterilisation does not require constant use of a contraceptive method, regular visits to health facilities or repeated expenditure on contraceptive supplies. Although sterilisation procedures usually demand a greater investment in skill, training and equipment than temporary methods of contraception, they provide lifelong protection against pregnancy, and are therefore more cost-effective. Since voluntary surgical contraception (VSC) procedures are almost always irreversible, clients require effective counselling before making any decision.

Mechanism of action

Voluntary surgical contraception (VSC) is a permanent family planning method, which involves female sterilisation or male sterilisation. In women, the process is called fallopian tube ligation or tubal ligation, and involves mechanically blocking the fallopian tubes by cutting them to prevent the sperm from reaching the egg. In men, vasectomy involves blocking the vasa deferentia, or sperm ducts, to prevent the passage of sperm into the semen, so that fertilisation and pregnancy during sexual intercourse cannot occur. You will see diagrams illustrating these procedures later in this study session.

Counselling for sterilisation

Sterilisation is a permanent method of contraception. Once the surgery has been performed, the individual cannot simply change his or her mind. A number of circumstances, usually hard to predict, may lead users to regret that the sterilisation procedure was performed, for example losing their children, getting divorced or remarried, or wishing for additional children.

Make certain that your client(s) correctly understand the procedure and its consequences. You must tell the client that VSC is irreversible. Once the client has undergone VSC it is extremely difficult for him/her to reverse the procedure and have more children. You can use the 'BRAIDED' concept for successful counselling, which you covered in Study Session 3.

Techniques of sterilisation

There are a number of simple and safe techniques for male and female sterilisation (see Figure 9.2) that can be carried out usually as outpatient procedures in hospitals. Most clients will be able to go home on the same day, as post-operative problems are not common. Pre-operative preparation, which includes counselling, is extremely important to ensure the willingness of the client, and to minimise fears and regret.

Female sterilisation

Female sterilisation is a surgical intervention that provides permanent contraception for women who do not want any more children. It is a safe and simple surgical procedure. Female sterilisation is also known as Tubal Ligation (TL), or 'tying the tubes', as well as VSC. TL is the procedure most commonly done in Ethiopia.

Procedure

Tubal ligation (TL) is a surgical sterilisation technique for women, where the fallopian tubes are cut, or blocked with rings, bands or clips. This procedure closes the fallopian tubes, and stops the egg from travelling to the fallopian tubes where fertilisation takes place. It also prevents sperm from travelling up the fallopian tube to fertilise an egg (see Figure 9.3 for details). Sterilisation is effective immediately after the procedure. Tubal ligations are 99.5% effective as a birth control method.

Sexuality

Women are fully able to enjoy sex after a tubal ligation. Usually, hormone levels and a woman's menstrual cycle are not affected by sterilisation. The ovaries continue to release eggs, but they remain in the fallopian tubes and are re-absorbed by the body. Some women experience improved sexual pleasure, because they are less worried about becoming pregnant.

Advantages and disadvantages

The advantages and disadvantages of sterilisation for women are summarised in Table 9.1. Being aware of these can help you provide effective counselling to your clients.

Male sterilisation

Vasectomy is a permanent method of contraception for men, involving a minor surgical procedure where the vasa deferentia (singular: vas deferens), or sperm ducts, are cut and then tied or sealed (see Figure 9.4). This operation keeps sperm from mixing into the semen when men ejaculate. Without sperm, fertilisation of an egg cannot occur, and so pregnancy is prevented. In Ethiopia, vasectomies are usually done in hospital settings under aseptic (surgically clean) conditions. They are much simpler procedures than female sterilisation, and as a birth control method vasectomies are 99.9% effective.

Procedure

During a vasectomy local anaesthetic is used. The healthcare provider makes a small opening in the skin of the scrotum. This allows the sperm tubes, or vasa deferentia, to be seen and cut. The procedure itself takes about 15 minutes.

Men usually rest at the hospital after the procedure. When they return home, ice packs and painkillers can ease swelling and discomfort. It is recommended that men take two days' rest, and perform only light activities for a week. For two days, it is helpful to wear scrotal supports and not take a bath.

It may take a week for men to feel comfortable and ready for sexual activity.

Important! Vasectomies are not immediately effective. The sperm which was in the tubes before the operation still needs to be ejaculated.

Vasectomies are not immediately effective after the operation. The sperm which was in the tubes before the operation still needs to be ejaculated. This may take about a month, or 10–30 ejaculations. Therefore, it is important to use other forms of birth control until the remaining sperm are cleared from the tubes.

Similar to tubal ligation, vasectomy is a permanent sterilisation technique. In developed countries, reversal surgery is available, but not always effective. The reversal procedure rejoins the cut ends of the vas deferens, but it is not always successful.

Sexuality

Men are able to fully enjoy sex after having a vasectomy. Hormonal levels and the feeling of orgasm stay exactly the same. In addition, the amount of fluid men ejaculate does not noticeably change. Some men experience improved sexual pleasure, because they no longer have to worry about making their partner pregnant.

Advantages and disadvantages

The advantages and disadvantages of sterilisation for men are summarised in Table 9.2. Knowing these will help you provide effective counselling to your community.

Permanent birth control.

Requires no daily attention.

Does not affect sexual pleasure.

Less complicated than female sterilisation.

Not immediately effective.

Requires minor surgery in a hospital.

May not be reversible.

Possible regret.

Possible rejoining of the vas deferens.

Does not protect against STIs, including HIV/AIDS.

What Is the Cervical Cap?

A soft, deep, latex or plastic rubber cup that snugly covers the cervix.

Comes in different sizes; requires fitting by a specifically trained provider.

How Effective?

Effectiveness depends on the user: Risk of pregnancy is greatest when the cervical cap with spermicide is not Effectiveness Arrowused with every act of sex.

Women who have given birth:

One of the least effective methods, as commonly used.

As commonly used, about 32 pregnancies per 100 women using the cervical cap with spermicide over the first year. This means that 68 of every 100 women using the cervical cap will not become pregnant.

When used correctly with every act of sex, about 26 pregnancies per 100 women using the cervical cap over the first year.

More effective among women who have not given birth:

As commonly used, about 16 pregnancies per 100 women using the cervical cap with spermicide over the first year. This means that 84 of every 100 women using the cervical cap will not become pregnant.

When used correctly with every act of sex, about 9 pregnancies per 100 women using the cervical cap over the first year.

www.ingramcontent.com/pod-product-compliance
Lightning Source LLC
Chambersburg PA
CBHW071921290426
44110CB00013B/1433